BUILDING WHAT'S IN A PHOTO

Learn how to realistically design, plan, and model

Kalmbach Media

On the cover: Delaware & Hudson/Lehigh Valley run-through freight MA-2 throttles up to take Richmond Hill in 1973, and again in HO scale on Dominic Bourgeois' Delaware & Hudson Second Division layout. See the description on page 76. *Jim Odell, collection of Gardiner Cross (prototype); Dominic Bourgeois (model)*

Back cover left: Andrew Dodge shares insights for scratchbuilding steam locomotives from brass. *Andrew Dodge* **Back cover right**: John Ciesla was inspired by a scene in his neighborhood that he knew wasn't going to last to build a diorama of an interlocking on the Long Island Rail Road. *John Ciesla*

Kalmbach Media
21027 Crossroads Circle
Waukesha, Wisconsin 53186
www.KalmbachHobbyStore.com

Published in 2022
26 25 24 23 22   1 2 3 4 5

Manufactured in China

ISBN: 978-1-62700-878-5
EISBN: 978-1-62700-879-2

Editor: Eric White
Book Design: Lisa Schroeder

Library of Congress Control Number: 2021940974

CONTENTS

Introduction 3

Chapter 1 4
Building a wooden arched truss bridge
Bernard Kempinski

Chapter 2 10
Build an interlocking scene
John F. Ciesla

Chapter 3 36
Saving Peerless Tanning
Lou Sassi

Chapter 4 40
Modeling where rail meets water
Paul J. Dolkos

Chapter 5 48
Modeling an old station
Alex Belida

Chapter 6 52
Backdrops bring a snowy scene to life
Mark Dance

Chapter 7 62
Pop-up railcar scrapping
M.R. Snell

Chapter 8 76
Filling in the background
Dominic Bourgeois

Chapter 9 86
Building an offline customer
James McNab

Chapter 10 98
Diamonds in the tracks
Todd Hermann

Chapter 11 112
Building from inside out
Ron Hoess

Chapter 12 116
Building Fisherman's Wharf
Harvey Simon

Chapter 13 126
Scratchbuilding a brass locomotive
Andrew Dodge

Chapter 14 142
Engine no. 18 in Kingfield
Lou Sassi

INTRODUCTION

The genesis for this project is the long-running feature in *Classic Trains* magazine, What's in a Photo, put together by Jerry Pinkepank. These photos are a treasure trove of information about classic railroading.

Photography has always been an important part of model railroading. We use it to share our modeling with others, and we use it to inspire us.

This book is about the photos that inspire us. Sometimes, there's a scene we just have to see in three dimensions, so we go all out to re-create everything in the image. Other times, an image is a spark—to learn more, to head off in a new direction, to improve our modeling. Photographs are also reference materials, allowing us to see how things used to be, to see places and machines that no longer exist.

We've gathered some of model railroading's most talented builders to share their models and the images that inspired them. In some cases, it was a published scene that inspired a project. But some of these projects are based on photos taken by the authors, either because they knew they were seeing something they might want to model some day, or perhaps because they wanted to be sure to preserve a scene on film or as digital data for future reference. One project was inspired by Google Maps.

And of course, where one photo might have been the inspiration, often there were other photos that filled in the gaps—the far side of a building, parts that were in shadow, details that were different in the inspirational photo from what the modeler wanted to depict in his chosen era.

Perhaps some of these photos will inspire you to model these same scenes, but more importantly, the projects in this book may inspire you to find your own projects, sparked by photos you've found or taken yourself. We hope you'll be inspired either way.

CHAPTER ONE

Building a wooden arched truss bridge

By Bernard Kempinski // Photos by the author unless noted

The final O scale scene captures the look of the original photograph. I could not capture the topography of the southern ridge exactly as in the photograph as I had to allow for access to the main water shut off valve for the house, which is located behind the southern abutment of the bridge, just behind the daredevil on the plank. *Inset, Library of Congress*

WHAT'S IN THE PHOTO

1. Arched Truss: The USMRR built the arched truss to avoid the possibility that flash floods would sweep away the earlier trestle's wood pilings. The parts for the truss were prefabricated off site and assembled on top of the existing trestle without disrupting the flow of railroad traffic.
2. Rock Cliff: At the bridge site, the Potomac Creek has cut nearly vertical cliffs through a narrow ridge that the railroad followed.
3. Detritus from construction: The workers left heaps of scrap lumber from the construction of the truss and previous bridges. Eventually, soldiers would scavenge this wood for fuel or construction of temporary shelters.
4. Cribbing: Log cribbing filled with stones supported the bents of the earlier trestle. The USMRR did not choose to remove them when it built the truss.
5. Stone Piers: The USMRR used the existing stone piers to help support all the bridges it built at the site.
6. Potomac Creek and marshy ground: The creek flows though flatter, marshy land before it cuts through the narrow ridge. By 1863 the Union Army denuded the surrounding area of trees for construction of previous bridges.
7. Truss rods: Wrought iron truss rods provide tensile strength to the mostly wooden truss.
8. Laminated wooden arch: According to the bridge designer, Herman Haupt, the arch provides the static strength of the bridge while the truss protects the arch from variable loads.
9. Stone abutments: A portion of the stone abutment at the south end of the bridge is today the only surviving element of the older wooden bridges.
10. Dare devil on plank: This plank was a popular spot for daredevils to pose for photographs as several photos show men perched on it.
11. Stripwood trusses
12. "Lincoln Log" cribbing
13. Piers: 1/8" plywood covered in embossed plastic sheet
14. O scale daredevil

The arched truss railroad bridge at Potomac Creek, Va., which is a tributary of the Potomac River, was one of four bridges the United States Military Railroad (USMRR) built at that site during the American Civil War. The Richmond, Fredericksburg & Potomac Railroad (RF&P) built the original arched truss and stone piers before the war. That bridge was wrecked by the rebels as they retreated from the area in late 1861. The first bridge the USMRR built was the famous "cornstalk and bean pole" trestle bridge. Due to the vicissitudes of war, Union soldiers destroyed that bridge under Gen. Ambrose Burnside's orders in July 1862.

The USMRR installed a new trestle in the same spot in November 1862. In late March 1863, it replaced that trestle with the arched truss design seen in the photos. That bridge was probably burned by rebels after the Union Army left to fight in the Gettysburg campaign in the summer of 1863. In June 1864, the USMRR built yet another trestle over Potomac Creek, which it operated for about two weeks. Then the railroad abandoned it as Gen. Ulysses S. Grant and the Army of the Potomac moved toward Richmond. Some time later, Confederate patrols destroyed that abandoned bridge.

From 1902 to 1907 the RF&P double-tracked the entire line with reduced grades and wider curves. As part of that project it built a steel girder trestle adjacent to the site of the original wooden truss bridge. Only a portion of one of the stone abutments remains today.

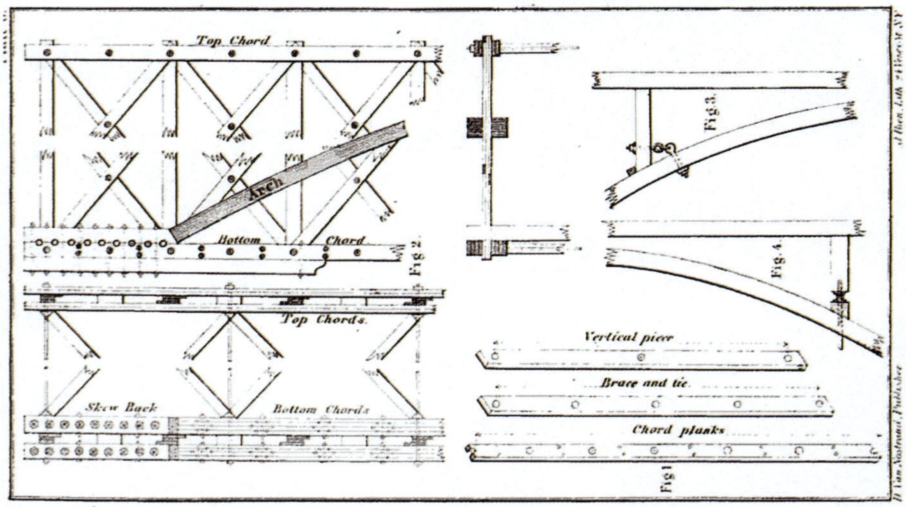

This drawing came from Herman Haupt's book on military bridges that he wrote after the Civil War. It shows construction details for the arch truss similar to the one at Potomac Creek.

I used a laser cutter to fabricate most of the wooden bridge parts. To assemble the truss, I used the top and bottom chords as a jig. The diagonal truss members fit precisely in the holes in the chords thanks to the accuracy of the laser cutter. The laser cutter was indispensable in this project as there were over 3,000 individual pieces.

SELECTIVE COMPRESSION

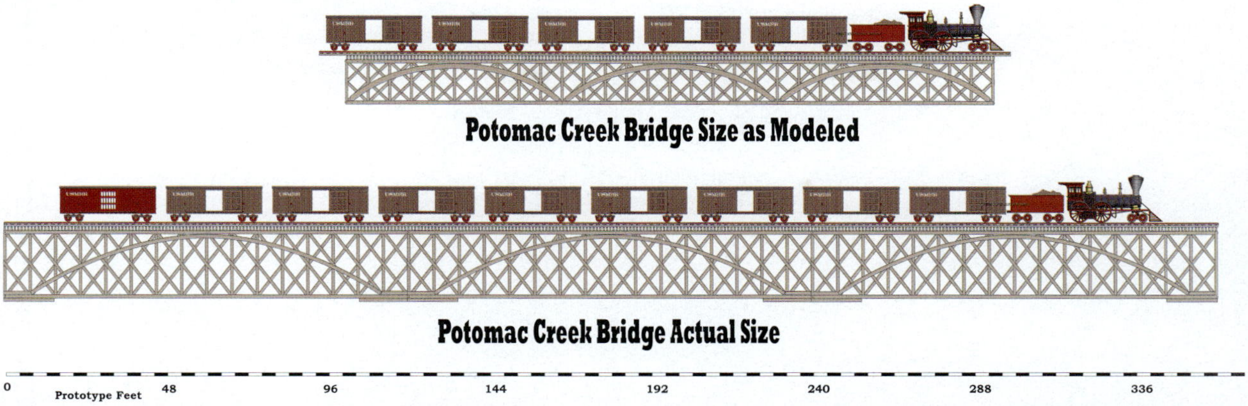

A problem sometimes encountered in building model railroad structures is how to shrink it down to make it fit the available space and still look like a believable structure. Model railroaders call this process "selective compression." My O scale bridge is about 52 percent of the actual bridge in length, but 75 percent in height. Each individual part had to be adjusted to match the prototype dimensions and fit into the selectively compressed bridge.

It took me three iterations of bridge truss panel construction to selectively compress the bridge to fit my site. In my first attempt, I built the first panel of truss scaled down by 50 percent, both in overall layout and individual members. That kept the overall look correct, but I was concerned that the truss members were too delicate looking for a railroad bridge.

The completed arch truss is quite strong and can cross the whole gap without sagging. However, I added the abutments and piers to maintain the prototype look. I built up the arches using a single piece of plywood, then covered the outside surfaces with individual boards cut so that the wood grain was oriented correctly. The truss rods are .032" brass rod I chemically etched to look black.

I used similar techniques to make the abutments and piers. First I cut away the existing rock terrain. Then I built a core structure of ⅛" plywood to fit the available space.

Once the cores for the abutments were properly sized, I covered them with embossed plastic sheets from Ratio's line of embossed plastic sheets.

I cut the cores for the piers from ⅛" plywood on the laser, ensuring the piers had the proper batter (slope).

To secure the embossed sheets to the cores I used cyanoacrylate adhesive (CA). To fill the gaps between the stone sheets I used a slurry of CA and baking soda. The slurry had a rough texture that matched the embossed stones.

The wooden supports on the top of the bridge are wider than the stone piers to match the prototype photos. I used various grays, browns and black to paint individual stones.

I tried making the log cribbing from sticks, but they were not straight enough. So, again I used my laser to cut the logs from ¼" basswood. I made them with notches like toy Lincoln Logs so they stacked nicely and had the correct batter.

To make the logs look more like real timber rather than laser cut basswood, I used a rasp to round the corners and add texture to simulate bark. I installed the cribs in place and filled the interior with stones.

PHOTOGRAPHS FROM THE CIVIL WAR

The Civil War was not the first war where a camera recorded images of the conflict. That happened in the Crimean War in the 1840s. By the time of the American Civil War, photography had become more widely available, though still somewhat of a novelty. Dozens of photographers worked in studios and in the field making images of civilians, military personnel, equipment, activities, and the aftermaths of battles.

Andrew Russell, seen standing on the steps in the photo at the right, was one of these photographers.

Russell was an accomplished artist prior to becoming a captain in the Union Volunteer Army. He became affiliated with USMRR when his unit was stationed in Alexandria, Va. He painted some of the landscape scenes on USMRR locomotives, such as on the engine *McCallum*, while in Alexandria.

He became interested in photography and learned the techniques during the war from a civilian photographer using a borrowed camera. Herman Haupt arranged to have Russell removed from his regiment to take photographs of Haupt's railroad projects to illustrate his reports on USMRR activities and promote his activities. Russell later went on to photograph construction of the transcontinental railroad, including the famous "Champagne" shot of the Golden Spike ceremony. It is possible that Russell was the first railfan photographer.

Because the wet-plate collodion negatives used at that time required from 5 to 20 seconds' exposure, there are no action photographs of the war. Despite the slow exposure, the large plates were able to capture amazing detail.

That detail can be seen in the high-resolution scans of the images available from several online archives.

There are about 6,000 images from the Civil War in the Library of Congress and U.S. National Archives. Many of them are portraits of people taken in studios. There are a handful of other images scattered across libraries, university archives and historical societies. It is a rare treat to find a previously unseen image when searching those sites.

Andrew Russell, standing, right, photographed the Civil War before he was hired by the Union Pacific RR, for which he photographed the Golden Spike ceremony in Utah.

Thus, we have a limited selection of railroad images to guide our modeling efforts. Thanks to Haupt and Russell, we have several artistically composed photographs of the USMRR in Virginia for the time period I model.

CHAPTER TWO

Build an interlocking scene

By John F. Ciesla // Photos by the author

The photo of Nassau Interlocking that inspired this project was taken in 1972. It looks east from beneath the old Mineola Boulevard Bridge, which was being shorn up with steel beams as it was in a state of imminent collapse. Of interest to the right of the photo are the remains of the old right of way to the Garden City secondary track (Originally called the Hempstead Branch of the LIRR, as compared to the line of the Central Railroad of Long Island) that went south to Garden City to a major junction with the Hempstead Line.

The HO scale scene is not an exercise in ultra-high-detail scratchbuilding or extensive kitbashing. Components used were primarily "off the shelf" items (or kits), which match as closely as possible the actual structures and components in the scene. Some of the kits used are obsolete, and required some effort to locate on the secondary market (i.e. eBay and swap meets). Yes, there was some kitbashing, and also some rearranging and repainting of parts in kits to make the scene look real, but none of it is overly complex or expensive to do.

WHAT'S IN THE PHOTO

1. Mineola Boulevard Bridge: The old Mineola Boulevard Bridge was erected in the 1920s and torn down around 2000 and replaced by a modern structure. This was a north-south concrete and steel bridge, carrying a major highway across the tracks, and was in fact one of the very first highways to cross over the LIRR main line. It was built around the same time as the current Mineola station and station plaza area. The highway bridge also provided the only pedestrian crossing of the LIRR tracks at the station.

2. Garden City Secondary: The secondary track curved sharply to the south from a turnout located at the Mineola Boulevard Bridge and then along the west wall of the Mineola traction power substation. The line was once used to bring solders to Camp Mills in Garden City during World War I, and was also used to service the once huge Queens County (later Mineola Fair Grounds) agricultural fair grounds.

3. Brick Substation (no. 8): Between the Garden City secondary and Main Street is the large traction power substation built in 1910 to supply power for the third rail along the main line, as well as the Garden City and Hempstead branches. It also supplied power for the third rail on the Oyster Bay Branch as far as East Williston (1934). The first mainline electric trains did not arrive in Mineola until 1926 with the extension of electrification from the Queens border.

4. Nassau Tower: Here again is another interesting piece of history. The current wooden tower was erected very quickly in early 1923 as the previous brick tower built in 1890 was demolished on New Year's Eve 1922 when an Erie boxcar derailed and crashed into the tower after picking the facing-point switch at the Oyster Bay branch (or perhaps the Garden City Secondary).

5. Main Street crossing: This crossing is just to the east and alongside Nassau Tower. It is a complex crossing as it includes the turnout frogs and diamond crossover to the Oyster Bay Branch. The maintenance of the crossing must have been a constant headache for the railroad, as it is both a high-traffic vehicle crossing and sees well over 100 trains a day. In the early years it was an earth and wood crossing, then replaced by wooden planks, and later wooden edging with asphalt filler. The crossing has been protected with gates for most of its existence, first by manual gates operated by crossing tenders (up until the 1950s), and then by automatic gates and flashers.

6. Atlas code 100 track and turnouts are also used (It must be noted that the geometry of the Atlas track will differ somewhat from the prototype).

7. Electrified third rail

8. Signals

9. Power distribution lines from the substation

10. High-tension pole lines along the right of way

I have lived near the Long Island Rail Road's Mineola station for the past 40 years and just to the east of the station is the historic "Nassau" interlocking where the two-track Oyster Bay Branch joins the two-track main line.

In just a few hundred feet (between the Mineola Boulevard Bridge and the Main Street crossing) lies an amazing amount of interesting railroad detail that lends itself to a small compact diorama, perfect for this project. Now is also the perfect time to do a project such as this, as this scene is about to disappear in the name of progress. The massive third track project, already well underway, will change the landscape here in Mineola. Several major elements of the scene will be torn down to make way for the third track. Nassau Tower and the old brick substation along Main Street will be torn down, and the Main Street crossing will also be forever gone.

For the creation of this HO scale scene I concentrated on that small area to the east of the Mineola Boulevard Bridge, and we will also go back in time to an earlier Mineola in the 1950s to early 1970s.

Follow along as I build this diorama that will preserve a bit of my local history.

Basic structure & layout

1. The space goal of this project was to "keep it small" and concentrate on that very interesting section between the Mineola Boulevard Bridge and the Main Street crossing, and if possible include one or more of the maintenance-of-way buildings at the junction, just to the east of Main Street.

As this was not going to be included on my current layout, I built it as a display module of a very modest

MATERIALS

Structure:
- 1x3 pine lumber cut as required
- ⅝" Homasote 16"x36" thick
- 1¼" wallboard screws
- ⅛" thick hardboard (fascia panels) Cut as required

Track and roadbed:
- Atlas RH no. 4 turnout, code 100 no. 0282
- Atlas LH no. 4 turnout, code 100 no. 0281 (2)
- Atlas crossing, 12½ degree, code 100 no. 0177
- Atlas flextrack, code 100 no. 0168
- Atlas rail joiners no. 0170
- Atlas track nails no. 2540
- Cork roadbed slab, Midwest Products no. 3030 11¾" x 36" x 3⁄16"
- Model Master, Afrika Mustard no. FS30266
- Model Master, Light Earth no. FS30140
- Model Master, Euro 1 Gray no. FS36081
- Tamiya Spray, Dull Red no. TS-33

size: 16 inches deep x 36 inches long. The structure was a basic frame of 1 x 3 lumber with two intermediate cross members for support. These were then screwed (1¼" wallboard screws), and glued together carefully to maintain 90 degree corners. Each section was clamped together and pilot holes were drilled to maintain a good fit for the screws. The top was constructed using Homasote screwed to the frame, again using wallboard screws.

2. With the basic frame ready, it was time to set it aside and lay out the scene. I again used a well proven method used during the design of my three Eastport Branch modules, laying out the track and structures full scale on a sheet of heavy brown paper.

With the small size of this project, this was going to be easy, or so I thought. I found a nice smooth sheet of 1/8" plywood in the basement 36" long x 24" wide and taped the paper to it, giving me a smooth working surface. I then began to rough out the track centers for the LIRR two track mainline (2" spacing), and then temporarily placed the three turnouts in position to get an idea as to how this was all going to work out.

I also made up cardboard place holders for the major structures (The substation and Nassau Tower) along with the Mineola Boulevard Bridge and Main Street crossing to see how these would fit in the scene.

I was immediately confronted by one of the basic laws of physics: "You can't get 10 pounds of potatoes into a 5-pound bag." I also found that the Garden City secondary track would not fit using a standard 18" radius curve, as the track would run right into the side of the substation, and the substation would also have to be selectively compressed (this would require a bit of additional kitbashing).

For the Garden City secondary, a 16" radius curve would work, and would still look passable as this was a very sharp turn in reality. Combined with a slightly compressed substation one problem was solved.

Next, the east end of the module was examined, where I had hoped to be able to show some of the maintenance-of-way shacks in the junction. Even using no. 4 turnouts it was simply not going to be possible to show these shacks at the junction, and still make it look close to the actual track plan. Moving Nassau tower and the substation slightly to the east and right alongside the turnouts worked out perfectly and placed the Main Street crossing at the right place. But the idea of having any of the maintenance-of-way shacks was gone. After these moves the proportions were about right for the scene, and there was also just enough depth (16") for the scene to look good. Once again, the full-size mockup worked to save time and frustration later on in the construction process.

3. Now that the paper layout phase was completed, it was time to transfer that information to the module's Homasote top. This was an easy task by just transferring the measurements full scale from one board to another. It was once again time for another "test fit" to assure all the structures would fit, and indeed they did.

With the layout now on the Homasote,

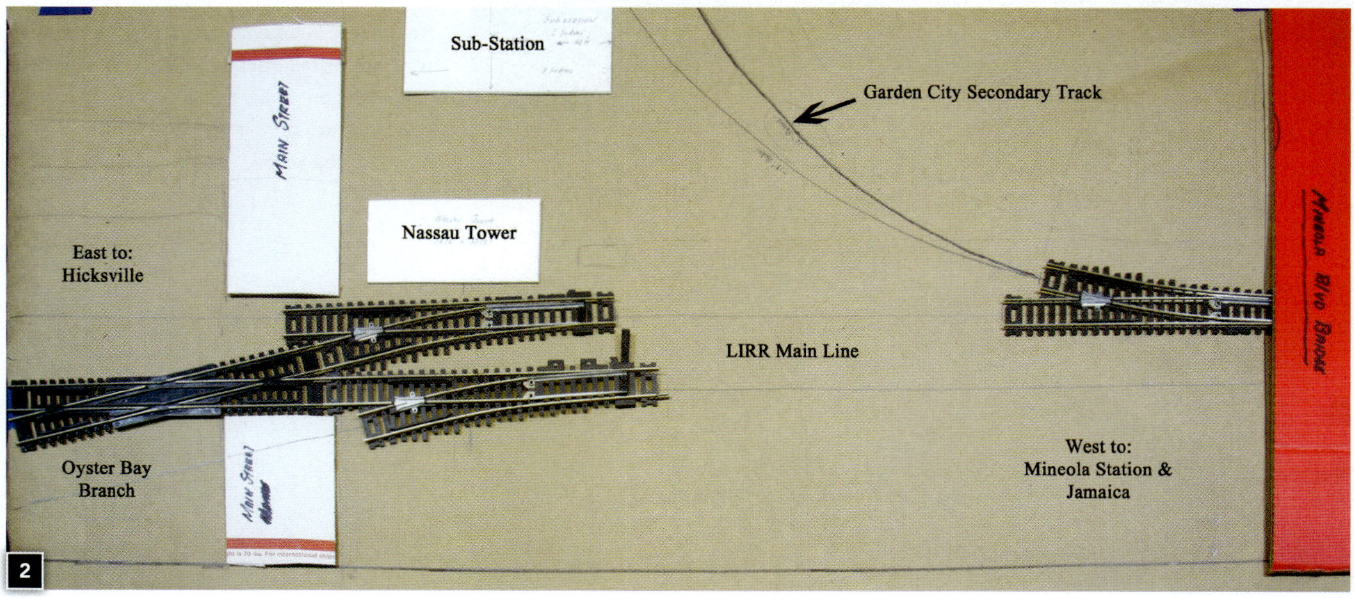

cutting the cork roadbed sheet was the next task. I used a large sheet rather than individual sections as I could include both mainline tracks, and the Oyster Bay branch tracks on a single piece, which greatly simplified the task of laying roadbed. I was also able to slightly widen the roadbed to allow for the tie extensions for the installation of the LIRR's electrified third rail.

The Garden City secondary was made by cutting the remaining cork roadbed into strips with beveled edges, so they could be bent around the sharp 16"-radius curve coming off the main line.

3

4

5

4. Next I went back into the workshop area to weather the track and turnouts before I installed them. As this would be a rather small module, I stayed away from the airbrush and instead use a combination of whatever spray can paints I hand on hand. I used four different spray paints to duplicate these details starting with the Tamiya TS-33 Dull Red to give the rails a bit of an oxide red base color (This is what I had on hand, other paints that give a rust hue will work as well). This was followed by sprays of Model Master FS30140 Light Earth aimed directly down to hit the ties. That was followed by Model Master FS36081 Euro 1 Gray, which was sprayed at a low angle to hit primarily the sides of the rails. This was finally followed by several shots of Model Master FS 30266 Afrika Mustard to give the effect of the pumping joints where mud had splashed onto the ties and rail. The intent here is not to completely layer the track with color over color, but to instead vary the color in short increments as with real track.

5. With the track painted and the cork roadbed secured to the Homasote, it was time to install the track and turnouts onto the roadbed using rail nails through the plastic ties of the Atlas code 100 track. With the rail weathered it was now difficult to know that this was the most basic of track systems as the look of "plastic" was completely gone. With the rails in place, the tops were polished with a very light abrasive, 600-grit sandpaper pad to get the rails clean.

Since this module is a standalone display item, there will be no need to solder power wires, or install insulated rail joints. Another simplification! I now set this aside and concentrated on the major structures that make up the scene.

Substation construction

MATERIALS

Design Preservation modular parts (Woodland Scenics):

- Powerhouse windows, no. 30118, 2 packs
- Two-story blank wall no. 30111, 1 pack
- Two-story rectangular 2 windows low no. 30137, 1 pack
- Cornice plain or no. 30117, 1 pack or
- Cornice fancy no. 30114, 1 pack
- Tamiya Hull Red no. XF-9
- Model Master Intermediate Blue spray no. FS35164
- Floquil Foundation no. F110084
- Evergreen styrene .040" black sheets no. 9115
- Evergreen styrene .030" white sheets no. 9030 used for bracing
- Evergreen styrene .125" square no. 186, .125" used for bracing
- Evergreen styrene angle no. 294, ⅛" (.125)
- Tamiya plastic cement extra thin
- Pan Pastels for weathering: grays, grime & soot, and rust & earth

From the scrap box:

- Central Valley bridge girder sections

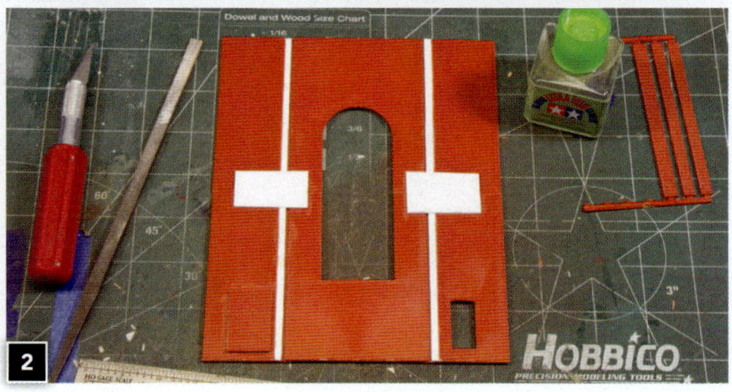

1. The substation is constructed of Design Preservation modular brick building parts modified to more closely resemble the LIRR structure. Photos of the more than 100-year-old building show that the bricks have weathered over time to an almost black color, and the large window frame structures are covered in a copper oxide color. Because of its size, the building will be compressed in its width in order to fit in the space between the Garden City secondary and Main Street.

2. I compressed the building horizontally by slicing the two story wall sections (DPM 30111, 30137) in half and using them on each side of one of the Powerhouse Window sections (DPM 30118). I later found the Powerhouse Window sections were also too tall for the substation, so I removed an 11 scale foot section from both windows and the lower brick sections. The point fell on a horizontal mullion in the window, and makes it look nearly identical to the windows of the LIRR Substation. The depth of the substation will be only one window section deep to fit the space available.

3

4

5

6

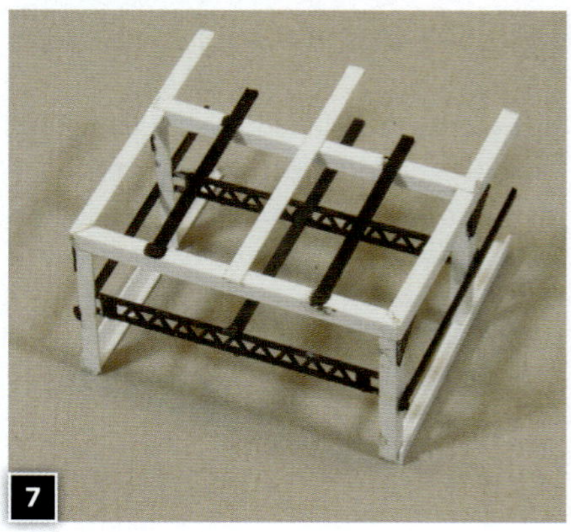

7

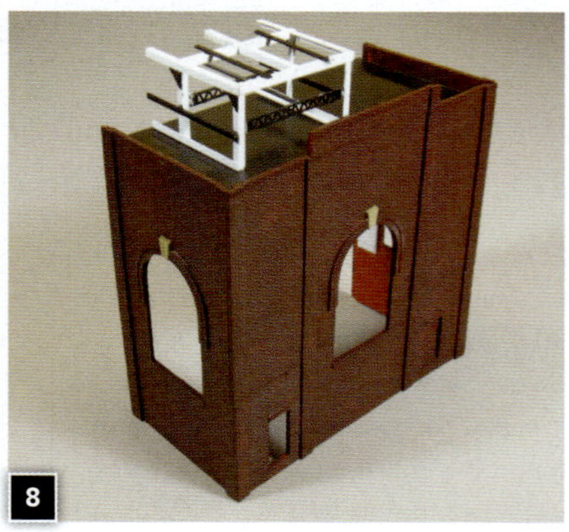

8

3. Note that when I assembled the building I did not realize the height of the DPM Powerhouse Window modules would not be proportionally correct for the substation until after assembly.

4. I had to perform a very precise razor-saw operation removing 11 scale feet of brick walls for the lower sections, then re-square the structure and glue it back. It is far easier to remove the 11 scale feet before assembly!

5. Once the parts are modified, they can be assembled in a straightforward manner as shown in the accompanying photos. Since the building will be used as a building front, the sections need to be braced to remain square, and have adequate support for the additional roof structure.

6. The structure can then be painted in a very dark brick color (Tamiya Hull Red, XF-9), and then windows and glazing can be added.

7. The roof is made of .040" Evergreen black styrene sheet fastened to .125" square styrene I used to brace the DPM wall section modules. On the roof is another interesting bit of structure, an open steel structure of various angle shapes, and some remaining high-tension cable insulators that appear to have been used in the past for the termination of various types of electrical cables.

8. I learned that was indeed the case, and was a common part of all older style traction power substations. The rooftop structure was used to secure high voltage transmission lines to the building and provide an entryway for those lines into the substation for eventual conversion to third rail traction power. In the early part of the 20th century there were few sources for the 11,000-volt, 3-phase, 25-cycle power used to feed the substations, so the railroad provided its own high-tension lines along the rights of way with taps to the various substations.

Nassau Tower

A primary goal of this part of the project was to find an off-the-shelf model that would resemble the prototype Nassau Tower as much as possible. I found there is no plastic kit currently in production that resembles Nassau Tower. Perhaps the closest kit in production is the Alexander Scale Models B&O Interlocking Tower kit (A-7880). This wood kit is intended for more advanced modelers.

1. A search of products on eBay did find a simpler alternative. An IHC Interlocking Tower kit no. 602 that had the proper shape of Nassau Tower (and appears to be the same prototype as the Alexander kit). It does however have a different window arrangement and had an external staircase on one side of the building that Nassau Tower does not have.

2. The wall sections are easily interchangeable, and by purchasing a second kit the better-matching wall section can be substituted (in my case I was able to find a bag of parts which included the wall needed). This same kit was also sold by AHM (no. 5825), and Tyco (no. 7773); there are plenty of these kits available on the secondary market.

3. This is a simple kit to assemble and with the substituted wall section yields a reasonable facsimile of the real Nassau Tower. Prior to assembly I painted the parts in colors that matched the prototype (flat primer white and Tamiya Dull Red spray). I sprayed the Dull Red first, shown being tested on an extra wall section. I allowed it to dry, then spayed the white primer over top.

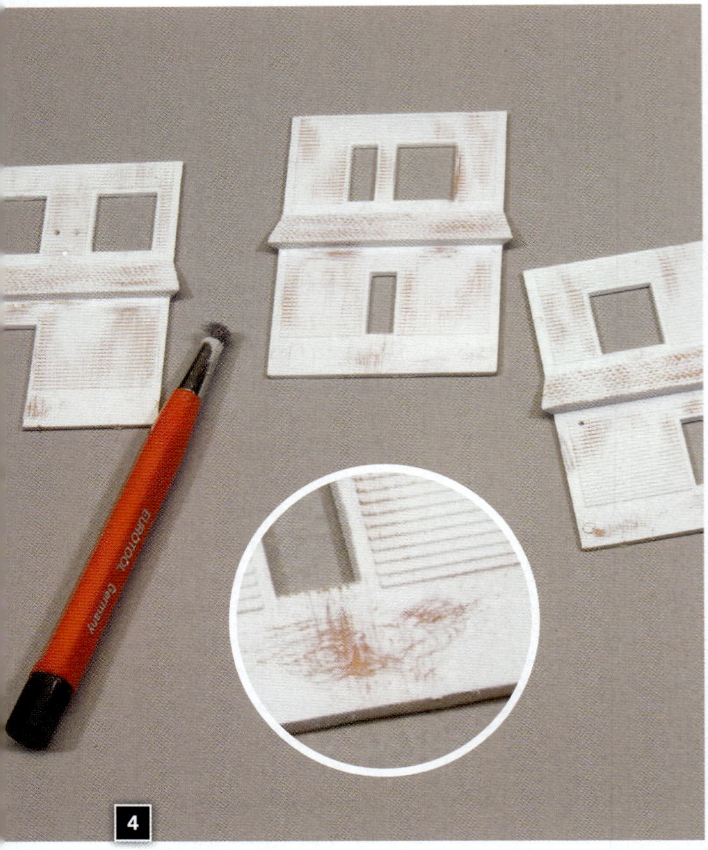

4

5

4. After both coats were dry, I used a micro wire brush tool to scrape through the white to reveal sections of the red, giving the look of peeling paint. The windows and trim were also painted Dull Red. The roof was painted Tamiya Hull Red (XF-9). The only modification done to the roof was to relocate the chimney from the side to the southeast corner as on the real Nassau Tower.

5. Other than those modifications, the structure was assembled according to the instructions, then weathered using Pan Pastels. Assembling the kit is very straightforward and simple. The kit also contains several additional parts that can be used in the final scene, including a cable reel, ladder, and an instrument case. These parts were painted and weathered as well.

6. Placing the completed "Nassau" tower next to the substation showed that the two buildings do work well together to make the scene (the IHC kit is a bit oversized for the actual Nassau Tower; however, most importantly, it is of the correct shape).

6

MATERIALS

- IHC Interlocking Tower kit no. 602
- Can also use: AHM no. 5825, Tyco no. 7773
- Flat white primer for exterior walls
- Tamiya Dull Red spray for windows and trim no. TS-33
- Tamiya Hull Red (roof) no. XF-9
- Tamiya Chrome-Silver (instrument box) no. X-11
- Tamiya Red Brown (ladder and cable reel) no. XF-64
- Floquil Oxide Red (chimney) no. F110186
- Floquil Weathered Black (chimney) no. F110017
- Pan Pastels (weathering) Grays, Grime & Soot, and Rust & Earth
- Wire Brush (micro) for scraping outer layer of paint
- Tamiya Plastic Cement extra thin
- For the more ambitious, use the Sheepscot Signal Tower w/Ball Signal and Crossing Shanty, no. 1030. This kit is no longer in production, but it can be found on the secondary market. The following additional parts were purchased for the project:
- Roof shingles, American Model Builders no. 285
- Interlocking machine, American Model Builders no. 388 (2)
- Tichy 30"x62" four-pane windows no. 8025 (match Grandt line no. 3215, GL5116)
- Tichy .37"x.36" small square window no. 8067
- Gap-filling CA
- Same paints/Pan Pastels as above

Nassau Tower version 2

For those wanting a bit more realistic Nassau Tower, that can also be done. Among my stockpiled old kits, I had a Sheepscot Boston & Maine interlocking tower kit (no.1030). Way back when, this kit originally retailed for $35, and compared to today's laser wood craftsman kits it is a bit of a dinosaur. The contents of the kit are in reality little more than a collection of scribed wood siding and several packets of scale lumber, plus Grandt Line windows, several small castings, and the instructions/plans.

It does however contain everything needed to construct an interlocking tower. By pushing the instructions aside and reconfiguring the walls and window arrangements, along with a vastly different roof structure, one has virtually all the parts necessary to construct an accurate Nassau Tower. I did the reconfiguration mostly by eye, using photos of the tower as references for dimensions of the building. Using wood for the structure does make for a better-looking finished model. Perhaps the most challenging and time-consuming part of the build was to lay the never-ending number of strips of roof shingles to the roof. I also was able to backdate the windows to an earlier configuration, which worked well for the scene.

To do this, additional windows were needed. If you cannot find the original Grandt Line windows, Tichy has virtually identical windows available in its catalog. The paint was the same as with the plastic kit. When completed, the structure will also contain an interior, with Saxby & Farmer interlocking levers.

Placing the two "Nassau" towers side by side the differences are apparent. However, both look like they belong in the scene, and that is the goal of this project.

Mineola Boulevard bridge

We will be building the old Mineola Boulevard Bridge, which was a steel and concrete structure erected in the mid-1920s and torn down around 2000. Had it not been finally taken down, it would have come down by itself, as it was in an imminent state of collapse. For the last five years of its existence it was shorn up with steel beams and additional columns. For many years water had leaked through the bridge structure, rusting and corroding the internal steel components.

However, the old bridge had some character, and that is the bridge that will be built. Also, since we are backdating the module to the 1960s, it's the one that was there. Photos of the old bridge are fairly numerous, and definitely show that overall clearance was tight, particularly for large locomotives such as the Alco C420s and later EMD GP38s.

This must be taken into account when building the bridge. This will be an exercise in scratchbuilding, as there is simply no off-the-shelf item that can be used for this. For construction materials we will go back to the dark ages of model railroad structure construction, and use illustration board and basswood as the primary components. Also, as the bridge is being used as the western edge of the module, it will not be full width, only the eastern sidewalk and one northbound traffic lane will be shown. The bridge will frame the western edge of the module. I did not have access to the original bridge plans, and since the original bridge is long gone, much of the measurements are done by the "eyeball" method.

MATERIALS

- 1/16" thick artists illustration board
- 1/8"-square basswood
- 1/8" x 3/16" basswood
- 1/32" basswood sheet (for sidewalk)
- Tichy Train Group, 3-rail pipe railing no. 1601
- Evergreen styrene H-columns no. 286 3/16" (.188")
- K&S brass rod no. 8160 (.032")
- 50/50 mix of Foundation and Sand paints no. F110084 Floquil, no. FS33531 Model Master
- Pan Pastels for weathering Grays, Grime & Soot, and Rust & Earth
- Wood filler or Squadron putty
- Pin vise with .033" drill bit
- Gap-filling CA
- Woodland Scenics Scenic Cement S191
- Woodland Scenics, Coarse Turf Medium Green T64, and Dark Green T65

Construction began with measuring 2"-wide sections of illustration board for the main span and for the southern approach ramp.

These sections are reinforced using 1/8"-square or 1/8" x 3/16" basswood strips. The main span sections include two groups of vertical styrene H columns on either side of the right of way.

The columns were attached with cyanoacrylate adhesive (CA) to 1/2" x 3/8" wooden sections representing concrete footings, then fastened to the underside of the main span.

At the north end of the bridge, a heavy duty support was made of 1/16" thick basswood sheet lined with 1/8"-square basswood to provide a support which will be hidden behind the fascia panel. After all components were assembled the section was sanded smooth and set aside.

5

The southern approach ramp to the bridge constructed of illustration board, and reinforced with ⅛"-square basswood. It was shaped to slide under the main span to provide support and also to begin a downgrade section for the highway off the bridge. Photos of this section show there were some added architectural items to add strength to the structure and enhance the overall look. There are several buttresses added along this section, the first one being where the approach meets the main span.

6

These add interest to the model and are not particularly difficult to build. I took a section of illustration board and cut it 3 scale feet wide, and glued it to the upper portion of the structure. The bottom 9 feet of the buttress projects outward from the structure at an angle. This can be done by adding a small 1⁄16"-piece of square stock between the structure and the bottom portion of the illustration board and using CA to hold everything in place. The open space was filled with either wood filler or Squadron Putty and sanded. Additional architectural details can be made simply by cutting sections of illustration board to outline the concrete sections.

7

Once the two sections were at this stage they were test-fitted onto the module to assure the components line up, and that the bridge columns have adequate clearance with the right of way. Once a good fit is assured, they were cemented together to form the complete span.

8

The sidewalk sections along the full length of the top of the bridge were next. I used the 1⁄16"-thick basswood for the sidewalk. I scribed sidewalk slab joints into the board, along with the curb. The sidewalk was then glued to the bridge with CA. Note that due to the curvature of the bridge the sidewalk sections need to be held in place to assure a strong bond.

9

Then it is time to place the concrete side barrier over the sidewalk on the main span. I cut the concrete slabs about 5 feet high and 8 feet in length each. Each slab is fastened to vertical uprights using .032" brass rod and spaced at 8-foot intervals.

10

The concrete slabs are two sections. The outer slab is a continuous strip of basswood about 5 scale feet high made from 1⁄16" sheet. At every 8-foot interval I scribed a vertical line where the brass rod was fastened into the bridge surface and along the outer slab.

11 I then added the scale 7'-9" inner slab sections, made from 1/32" basswood, on the inside, allowing space for the vertical wire supports.

12 Finally, 1/16"-thick x 1/8" strips were added to cover the slab joints to look like the concrete vertical uprights. This will add the necessary strength to these sections. I maintained a 1/32" gap between the top surface of the sidewalk and the bottom of the side slabs.

On the approach span there are no concrete side slabs. Instead the bridge is lined by pipe railings up to the main span (Tichy pipe railings no. 1601).

13 Painting the structure seemed like the easy part. However, selecting the right color was a challenge. I wanted to use Floquil Aged Concrete (no. F110016), which is no longer produced. I didn't have enough left in the bottle to do the entire bridge structure. After several attempts, I arrived at a 50/50 mix of Floquil Foundation (no. F110084) and Model Master Sand. The roadway and vertical H columns were painted using the remains of a bottle of Floquil Weathered Black (F110017).

14 Next was applying the weathering. The bridge had many leaks and was deeply stained by rust and diesel exhaust soot from the LIRR Alco locomotives, well known for their dramatic exhaust when accelerating out of a station. There were also a lot of calcium carbonate deposits on the bridge from the concrete dissolving as water mixed with vehicle and diesel exhaust, which also created stalactites growing down from under the structure. I used paint (oxide red) for the rust stains, and heavy weathering using Pan Pastels for the exhaust stains and deposits on the concrete.

15 Photos of the southern approach ramp also show that there was a large growth of ivy extending from the ground level all the way up to and including some of the hand railings. This was replicated by using a thin brush to apply scenic cement in veins along the side of the bridge, and then sprinkling dark green ground foam on the still-wet cement.

Terrain

MATERIALS

- White foam core board, 3⁄16" thick
- Carpenter's glue
- Pre-mixed patching plaster
- Various colors of acrylic artist's paints for terrain

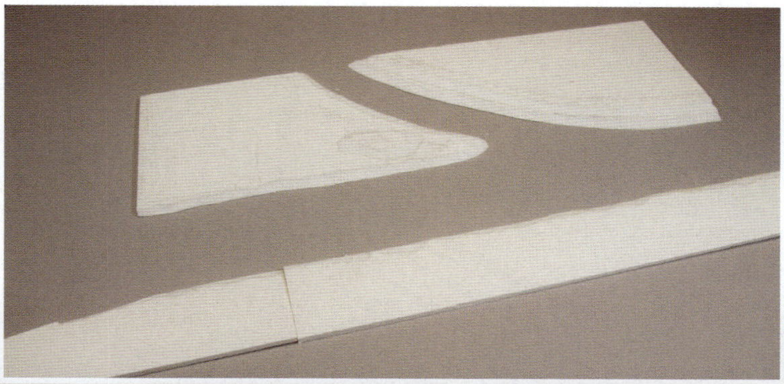

With the track in place on the module, it was now time to add the scenic contours to the scene. Nassau Interlocking in Mineola is on relatively flat terrain as it is on what was once the largest grassland east of the Mississippi, the Great Hempstead Plains.

However, even with a relatively flat surface there are still variations in the elevation, and they add interest to the scene. To accomplish this, a sheet of 3⁄16"-thick white foam core board was used to raise the ground level throughout the scene. In the area just to the east of the Mineola Bridge the foam core was doubled in thickness as photos show a parking area at a higher elevation. The foam core was cut to conform to the track layout, and was also used as a base for the surrounding roads in the scene.

All sections were test fitted, sanded smooth, then glued to the Homasote using carpenters glue. I used push pins and weights to hold the foam core until the glue dried. An application of painter's pre-mixed patching plaster was then used to cover the foam core and give a more realistic, textured appearance. The plaster was only slightly smoothed with minor carving as these areas would eventually be covered with grass, earth, or ballast.

Main Street crossing and terrain paint

1

2

1. I then turned my attention to the Main Street crossing. The crossing was typical for the 1950s through 1960s era and had timber edges (along the rail) with an asphalt fill. The crossing is complex as it includes two turnouts along with a crossover and the two Oyster Bay tracks coming off the main line at an angle.

2. I duplicated the timbers with basswood (1⁄16" x 1⁄8") and pre-mixed patching plaster for the asphalt. The roadway had to be raised slightly as it approached the rail height. I used pre-mixed patching plaster layered to the underlying foam core that I later painted to match the asphalt/concrete road surface.

3. With the crossing in place, the next step was paint. It has always been my standard practice to apply a coat of paint to all scenic terrain surfaces such as grassy and soil areas. The colors used approximate the same colors to be used when the final ground foam/materials are applied as the final surface. This covers all the white surfaces in the event any of the ground foam becomes dislodged.

I also painted the asphalt surfaces such as the parking lot, Main Street, and the section of Front Street south of the tracks at this time. The section of Front Street on the north side of the tracks was painted to represent concrete. The concrete sections have expansion joints scribed, then were given an India ink wash.

3

Crossing lights and gates

1

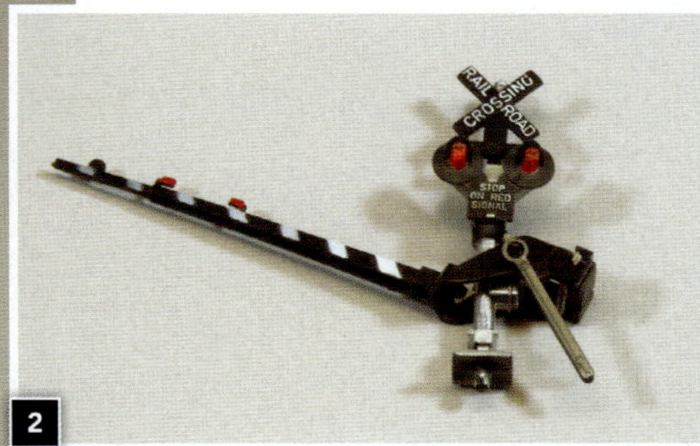

2

MATERIALS

- Tyco crossing lights and gates no. 908 (or) NJ International crossing lights & gates nos. 1161, 1163
- Tamiya Chrome Silver X11
- Model Master Guards Red 2718
- DAP pre-mixed patching plaster or equal
- Various colors of acrylic paints for crossing
- Dark wash for crossing boards: Dilute mixture of burnt umber, neutral gray no. 2 and flat black
- Basswood 1/16" x 1/8" wide

1. With the crossing painted, it is a good time to take a break from the module and prepare the Tyco no. 908 gates for later installation at the crossing. Operating crossing gates with lights are usually an expensive addition to a model railroad, and there are some excellently scaled and manufactured examples ready for purchase (for example, various items made by NJ International). However, for this application the gates and lights will not be functional. The old Tyco gates/lights have a plastic highway crossing base that is part of the kit. I was after only the lights and crossing gates. Although a very simple and basic part, it will be tuned up a bit to work well at the Main Street crossing.

2. Out of the box, the lights and gate assembly is a single part. However, it contains an actuator rod that needs to be removed from the gate arm (items 3 and 4 in the Tyco instructions). Also the gate arm and the light/sign assemblies are painted opposite to the colors used on the LIRR crossing. Long Island RR practice has been to have the gate arm, signs, light assemblies, and the mounting pole to be painted silver.

3. I remedied this with an application of Tamiya Chrome Silver. A simple trick is used to turn the "crossing" lettering black. I scraped a sharp blade across the lettering, removing the silver and the underlying white paint to expose the original black plastic surface (see before and after photo). This is also a good time to touch up the paint used for the lights on the crossing gate arms. I used a quick application of Model Master Guards Red paint. Set the gates aside for later installation on the crossing. The Tyco gates and lights are a bit oversized for HO.

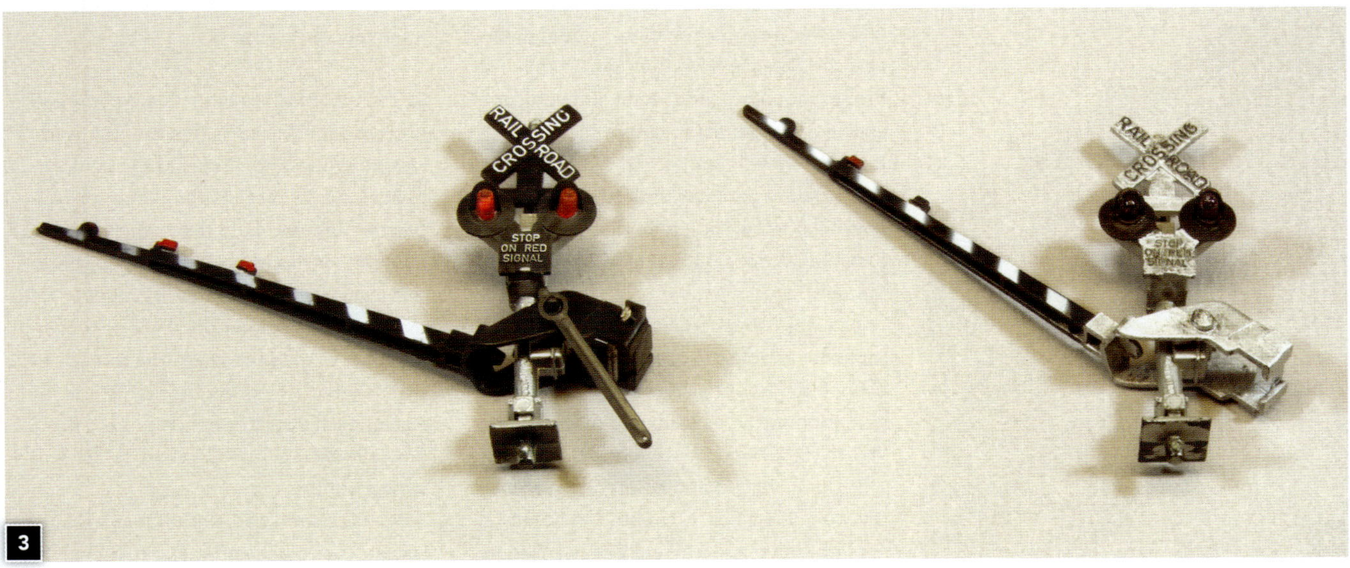

3

Construction and installation of third rail

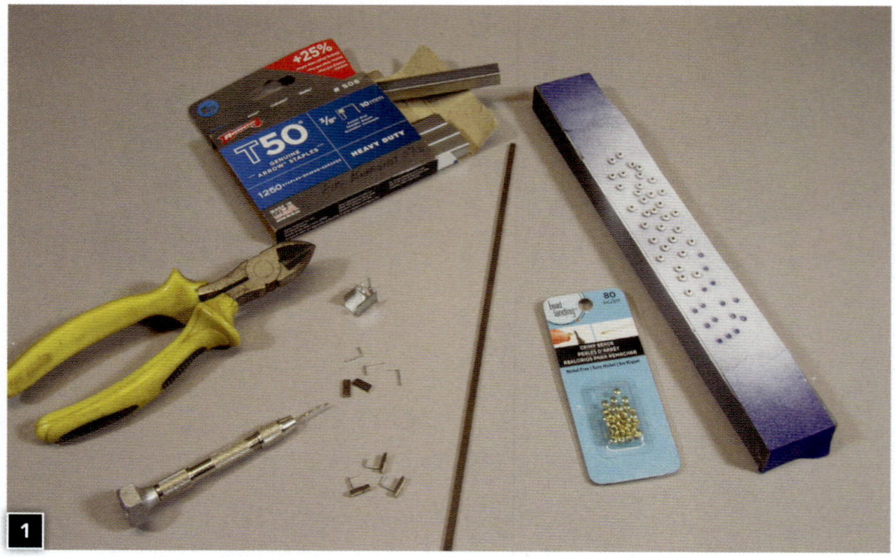

1

MATERIALS

- T50 3/8"-deep HD staples, Arrow no. 506 (or equal)
- Crimp beads, Bead Landing (purchased from Michaels)
- Basswood 1/16" x 1/4" wide
- Basswood 1/32" x 1/8" wide or ships planking
- Running rail for third rail Atlas code 83
- Walthers Goo
- Gap-filling CA
- No. 6 x 3/4" round-head wood screws (for potheads, see text)

2

3

1. This is perhaps one of the most tedious and delicate parts of the module and one of the most challenging, as there are no off-the-shelf third-rail assemblies produced. This requires scratchbuilding using some very basic and also unusual items. However, the reward is something truly unique once finished, as few model railroads can boast a third-rail installation.

The Long Island Rail Road uses an "overrunning" type of third rail where the pickup shoe rides above the third rail. This is the most common type of installation used by transit systems. The other major type is the "underrunning" where the pickup shoe rides under the rail.

2. Third rail ties are usually spaced at every fifth tie. These ties are a bit longer and allow for the third rail bracket, insulator, and cover board assemblies to be mounted at a set distance from the running rail. Proper mounting (horizontal and vertical spacing) is essential to assure that the third-rail shoes mounted on the equipment make good contact with third rail, and that rail equipment (car bodies and truck assemblies) does not come in contact with the rail.

As I was using common code 100 sectional and flextrack, I did not replace every fifth tie, but instead added an extension to the existing ties made from 1/16"-thick, 1/4"-wide basswood about a scale 2'-9" long stained and painted to match the weathered ties. I mounted the third rail assemblies to these extensions. I drilled a hole close to one end using a 3/64" drill in a pin vise. Use caution and let the drill do the work, otherwise you might split the wood. This hole will be used for mounting the third rail bracket.

The third-rail bracket is a common T50 staple, 3/8" deep. The staple is cut to size using heavy-duty wire-cutting pliers. I cut off one of the legs completely and cut the other about 1/8" long. It will be where the protection board will be mounted. I dipped the long side in CA, then pushed it into the hole in the tie extension. Make sure that each bracket (staple) is vertical, then allow the CA to harden.

I glued the tie extension/bracket assembly to the tie and roadbed using CA (Goo would work as well, but can be rather messy). It is important to firmly press each assembly onto the roadbed to assure a secure bond until completely dry. It is also a good time to run several pieces of rolling stock along the area to assure that there is adequate clearance.

3. The electrical insulator is a crimp bead, purchased at Michaels (the brand I used was Bead Landing). I placed the crimp beads on a strip of masking tape (or blue painters tape) to hold them, then sprayed them either flat white or flat sand. The full-size insulators were made of porcelain or glass and were either off-white or brown. I used CA to glue the insulators to each tie extension touching the bracket (staple). Again, each insulator needs to be held down firmly until the CA cures to achieve a strong bond.

At this point I had all the brackets and insulators in place and ready to mount the third rail. I used sections of code 83 HO running rail, as is it easily available and will approximate the height of the third rail more realistically (If one can find scale third rail, all the better). Each section of third rail needs to be measured and the ends need to be filed down at an angle to provide a run on and run off (also known as nose pieces) for the passing third rail shoes from the cars and locomotives. At this point it's also a good idea to solder the power leads to the third rail sections. Even though I was not energizing the sections, I still needed to show the connection to the third rail from the "pothead."

4

5

4. So the next question is, "what's a pothead?" No, it's not some spaced-out, groggy character propped up next to a building. In electrified railway lingo the pothead is the place where the underground power cable reaches the surface and is terminated at a connecting point.

Here a cable is connected and run to the third rail to provide a solid connection for traction power. A weatherproof cover (often a concrete casting) is placed over this connection to provide a weatherproof seal. This concrete cover looks much like an overturned pot, thus a "pothead." We will make that connection after the third rail is mounted.

The potheads are made from roundhead wood screws with the center slot filled with a strip of styrene and then filed smooth to give the proper shape. I drilled a small hole into the screw shaft just below the head where the power cable will be secured. With the third rail installed, all that is left is to install the potheads near the third rails by drilling a hole in the Homasote. I then ran the wire that was soldered to the third rail to the pothead and secured it under the screw head. There should be about a scale 4'-6" clearance between the bottom of the screw head and the ground.

5. Although I have used code 83 running rail for the third rail, it is the wrong cross section and is too tall. Electric traction third rail is a unique type of rail, and does not share a similar cross section to the far more common running rail. The basic shape is much like a very compact and dense "I" or "H" beam with the flat surfaces at the top and bottom. It is also very heavy, often exceeding the weight of running rail (of the same length) in order to carry the current needed to propel multiple-unit cars. I could have used N scale code 80 or 55 rail, which would have been lower, but that would have also been the wrong cross section. The code 83 does have a more massive look to it that I think is the best compromise.

Aged third rail is usually dark gray much like running rail, but is much less likely to have mud splashes as it is higher off the ground. Each section of third rail was painted and set out to dry. Once dry, I cleaned the contact portion of the rail as this surface is constantly being polished by passing third rail shoes.

The next step is to mount the third rail onto the individual insulators. I placed a small dollop of Walthers Goo (contact cement) on each insulator, then pressed the third rail in place. I prefer the contact cement to CA as the contact cement has a bit more flexibility and greater shear strength.

6

6. The final touch is adding the cover (protection boards) $\frac{1}{32}$" x $\frac{1}{8}$" basswood to the undersides of the brackets using small amounts of CA on the underside of each bracket. Again the boards need to be held in place until the glue cures (using tweezers). I had a supply of mahogany ship planking that worked well for these boards. This was then followed up by painting/staining of the boards to give them a well-weathered look.

Once again ensure that there is adequate clearance for equipment, and if so, you now have a realistic-looking third rail installation.

Ballasting and ground cover

1

MATERIALS

- Woodland Scenics, medium gray ballast no. B82
- Woodland Scenics, Scenic Glue no. S190
- Woodland Scenics, Scenic Cement or Matte Medium no. S191
- Woodland Scenics, Burnt Grass no. T44
- Woodland Scenics, Earth Blend no. T50
- Woodland Scenics, Soil no. T41
- Ballast wash, dilute mixture: burnt umber, neutral gray no. 2, Tamiya Black XF1
- "Wet water" mixture/spray bottle: Mixture of water and a few drops of dish detergent to reduce surface tension.
- Gloss medium
- Paint pipettes

1. I now moved to the next major portion of the project: ballasting the track and applying the primary layer of ground cover. I will not go into details as to how to ballast track and apply ground cover, as that has already been well covered over the years in numerous articles, along with the use of many different materials. Anyone who has performed this task uses the well proven process of applying an adhesive, spreading the material, and then sealing it in place, and after doing it several times we all add our own personal enhancements to the process.

Similar to most Eastern railroads, the LIRR has long used a light gray ballast on its main line tracks. Woodland Scenics Medium Gray Ballast is a good match.

Ballasting the track with third rail in place is a bit more difficult due to the delicate structure along the rails. I laid down a thick layer of Woodland Scenics Scenic Glue along the outsides of the track, being careful not to get glue on the third rail. I then carefully placed ballast on the sides and inside the gauge of the track. One of my favorite tools is a simple index card (or scrap piece of cardboard or styrene) I use to keep ballast in a straight line and keep it off already scenicked areas along the right of way.

After the ballast is placed, I follow up with a spray of wet water (water with a few drops of dishwashing soap mixed in so it will flow), then a careful application of Scenic Cement (or dilute matte medium) using a paint pipette. Then I stay away a good 16 to 24 hours to let the ballast dry.

Once the ballast is dry, the rails need to be cleaned of any ballast that has adhered to the inside of the rails, crossing and turnout flanges, and in the turnout's points. A small screwdriver blade usually works to loosen ballast. When I finished with that, I vacuumed the loose ballast. Then I ran a test car along the tracks to find any additional ballast interference.

2. The final act of laying down ballast is to give it a slight weathering to increase the depth and give it a better three-dimensional look. I brushed a very dilute mixture of burnt umber, neutral gray no. 2, and some Tamiya Flat Black (XF-1) onto the ballast with a wide soft brush. The effect creates an immediate increase in both depth and texture to the ballast. Vary the amount on the brush to create darker and lighter areas of ballast.

The same wash was also used to coat the tops of the third rail protection boards to give them a realistic weathered look. The old wooden protection boards were often a very dark brown (almost black) from being in the weather day after day, and many were broken and cracked as they aged.

3. With the ballast in place and dry, I began to apply grass and earth blends to the terrain sections of the module. This process is very much like laying down the ballast except instead of using a thick layer of Scenic Glue, I used Woodland Scenics Scenic Cement as the materials are much lighter than ballast.

Again, I used the index card to protect the newly installed ballast, areas such as roadways, and locations of structures. After applying the terrain materials, I sprayed the area with wet water and applied scenic cement to complete the task. Let the terrain blends dry for an extended time as it can be easily disturbed.

Low areas along the right of way accumulate standing water during passing rain storms. I applied gloss medium using a pipette to duplicate this effect. Typical locations are along the roadways and in sections past the ballast line in trenches.

When applying the gloss medium, do it slowly to reduce to possibility of air bubbles. If some appear, puncture them before the material dries. It will take a good 24 hours for the medium to dry, particularly if the application is relatively deep. Once dry, the gloss medium will remain clear and glossy, very much like standing water.

Application of scenic items

1

With the primary ground cover applied it is time for the next step, applying texture to the ground cover. I used photos as reference for the location of tall grasses, weeds, shrubs and trees, vines, and other organic materials, and began to apply the items as needed. Most of these items can be applied using Scenic Glue.

MATERIALS

- Bachmann Tufts, 6mm no. 31033 Tan
- Bachmann Tufts, 10mm no. 31041 Light Green
- Bachmann Static Grass (pull apart) no. 31014 Dry Grass
- Woodland Scenics, Scenic Glue no. S190
- Woodland Scenics, Scenic Cement or Matte Medium no. S191
- Scenic Express, Super Tree Armatures
- Woodland Scenics, Red no. 1355
- Woodland Scenics, Yellow no. 1353
- Woodland Scenics, Dark Red Rust no. 1356
- Woodland Sceincs Orange no. T1354
- Woodland Scenics, Green no. T1364
- Woodland Scenics, Natural Straw field grass no. FG171
- Unscented Hair Spray

2

I applied the tall natural straw field grass in the locations where there was standing water, which is a typical location for this type of grass. I placed 6mm and 10mm tufts near the edges of buildings, signal cases, and along the grassy areas. Pull-apart static grass works well along the edges of buildings and the Mineola Boulevard Bridge, and along fence lines where grass is generally not cut regularly. Do not overdo the applications, keep them light and airy so they look natural and do not overpower the scene.

3

I made the trees using painted Scenic Express Super Tree armatures with coarse ground foam applied, and planted in the scene (there have been numerous articles of tree making, and I'll not repeat an already well-covered process).

Most tree trunks are a shade of gray, not brown. Leaves can be of differing colors depending on the season. As this scene is being modeled in the autumn, leaves can be various shades of yellow, red, rust, and brown. From the photos of the scene there were medium-sized trees beside the substation and several scrawny trees along the concrete section of Front Street. On the south side of the tracks, Front Street has several trees along with some low "scrub" and dead tree debris to add interest to the scene.

Application of signals and details

Next I began applying the many detail items that will bring the module to life. Here again it is important to have photos of the area from the time period being modeled. Photos show many of the objects have either been replaced or moved with the passage of time. For example, the type and location of poles and attached signal and high-tension lines has changed several times, signal cases have been moved, and third-rail locations have moved. Many of the changes came about when the Garden City secondary track was removed from service, and when the Hicksville/Huntington electrification extension took place in the late 1960s.

Crossing gates

I installed the Main Street crossing gates, which were already painted and prepared in an earlier step, on both sides of the tracks. As is customary, the gate fixtures are mounted on the right side of the highway, close to the running tracks. The crossing is a bit complex as one is crossing four tracks (two main line and two Oyster Bay), and the highway is crossing at the locations of the switch frogs. I drilled a small hole and cemented the gate in place. If you carefully balance the gate arms, they can be positioned into either position for photos.

Signals

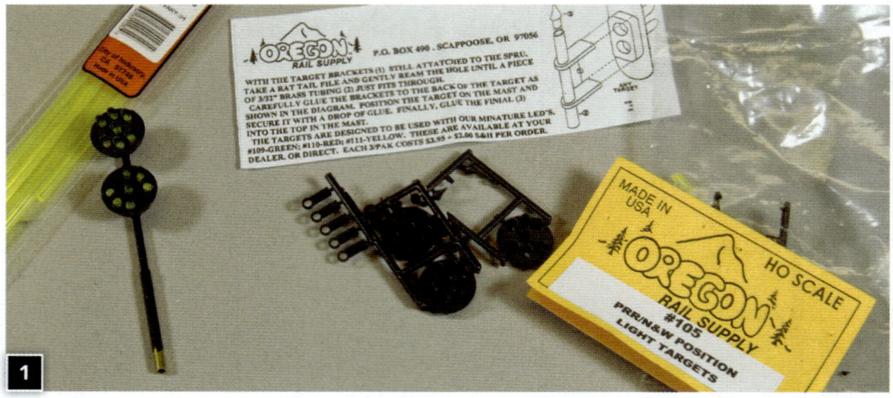

MATERIALS

- Oregon Rail Supply PRR/NW Position Light Signal Heads no. 105
- Plastruct Fluorescent Yellow Rods, 3/32" no. 90282
- K&S Brass Tubing 3/32" and 1/8"
- Gap-filling CA
- Tamiya Plastic Cement extra thin
- Walthers Goo
- Woodland Scenics, Scenic Glue no. S190
- Tamiya Flat Black XF-1
- Tamiya Buff (aged cement color) XF-57
- Thin scrap styrene sections

1. These are small but essential details which help to add considerable realism to the scene. Located alongside Track 2 just before Nassau Tower is a typical PRR two-head position light signal, and is essentially in the same location today. It is used to protect movements to the Oyster Bay branch, and along the main line eastward. Once again, as in the case of the crossing gates, scale signals are an expensive item and as this is a display module there is no need for a functional signal. A search on eBay revealed plastic position light signal heads made by Oregon Rail Supply (no. 105) that would be perfect. These signal heads are made to accept miniature light-emitting diodes and have openings in the head along with the sun shields.

To fill the openings, I found a package of Plastruct yellow fluorescent rods I could cut into fairly thin slices and make a perfect representation of the yellow signal lamps used by the LIRR/PRR.

I first ordered the signal heads, then measured the openings, which were about 3/32". I then ordered the matching rods. All that was required was to slightly ream the signal lens openings larger with a round needle file and then insert the fluorescent rod sections.

2. All that was left was to add the mounting brackets to the heads and insert 3/32" brass tubing for the mast. This was inserted into a 1/8" brass tube at the base. I glued the tubing together with CA, then painted the signals with Tamiya flat back XF-1. I drilled a 1/8" hole into the module at a location to match the photos, and glued the assembly in place with Scenic Cement.

3. When the Garden City secondary branch was still active, trains heading west off the branch were held by a dwarf signal. The signal was located just before the turnout from track 2 to the branch. Due to the sharp curve and the moves across the interlocking, this signal most likely showed nothing more than stop, slow clear, or restricting.

4. As with the home signal, it would have to be scratchbuilt. Fortunately, there were still several position light signal heads left over from the build of the home signal (Oregon Rail Supply no.105).

I selected the signal head based on the aspects that would have been displayed by this signal. I made a vertical and horizontal cut with a razor saw to produce the shape of a PRR type position light dwarf signal.

Like the home signal, I installed Plastruct yellow fluorescent rods as lenses for the signal. Using scrap sections of styrene, I added sides and a back to the signal head, then painted it Tamiya XF-1 flat black.

With the head complete, I mounted the signal on a concrete foundation the same width of the dwarf signal. I used .125"-square styrene. I painted the foundation Tamiya XF-57 Buff, which makes a good color for older concrete.

When I placed the dwarf signal, I kept in mind the track has a sharp curve, and the signal must be aimed slightly upward toward the locomotive cab to be visible by the locomotive engineer. I then cemented the dwarf signal to the ground using Scenic Glue

All that remained was to add a cast instrument case I found with my spare parts.

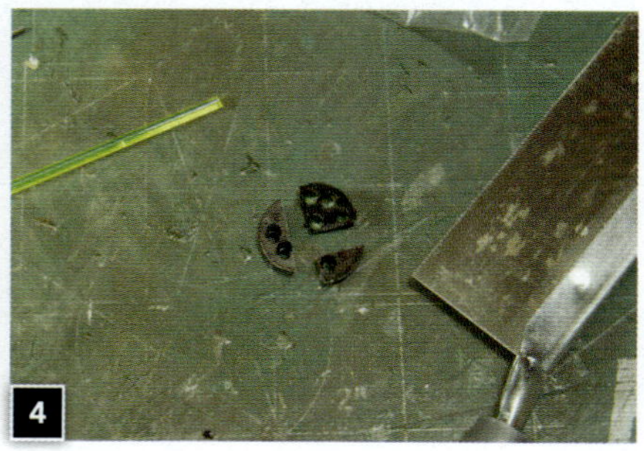

Parking lot fence

MATERIALS

- Chain Link Fence kit no. 933-3125 Walthers Cornerstone
- Gap filling CA and accelerator
- Tamiya Plastic Cement extra thin
- Woodland Scenics, Scenic Glue no. S190
- Aluminum or Dark Metallic Charcoal paint

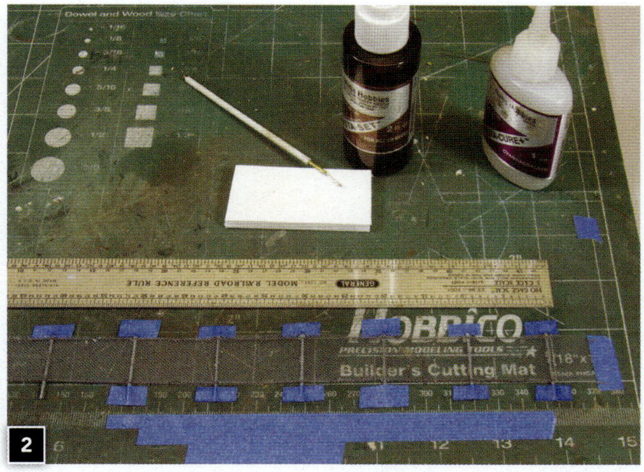

1. Photos of the old parking lot on the east side of the Mineola Boulevard Bridge show that an 8-foot-high chain-link fence was installed to separate the lot from the Garden City secondary tracks. Vegetation (weeds, vines, and small trees) grew along the fence, and it also served as a catchall for wind-driven debris such as old newspapers, and other typical castoffs.

I built the fence using the Walthers Cornerstone chain-link fence kit. It is important to line up and position the fence posts so they remain stationary during assembly. I used small sections of blue painters tape to hold the posts in position.

2. Unlike in the kit, the parking lot fence did not have barbed wire sections on the top, so I modified the posts. I glued the horizontal sections to the posts, staggering the joints to make the structure stronger.

Gluing the fencing material to the posts can be tricky. I kept the fence assembly taped to my work pad, and carefully placed the chain link material over the fence assembly. I taped one end to the work pad to provide a bit of tension while I stretched the material, then secured it along the posts and horizontal pipes with CA. I used CA accelerator to assist during this assembly process.

3. Although the instructions say to paint the materials before assembly, which I did, I still needed to respray the fence as a completed assembly to get a finished look. The instructions suggest using silver paint. However, I had an old can of automotive touchup spray paint that was a darker charcoal metallic. It looked far more realistic than a bright silver or aluminum color.

4. The fence curves around from the main line and follows the Garden City secondary tracks to the limit of the module. I placed the fence on the module by making a series of small holes spaced to match the fence posts. I secured it with Scenic Glue. The fencing material is very delicate, some of the joints will no doubt open up as it is placed on the scene, requiring a careful repair.

Front Street fence

MATERIALS

- Basswood 1/16" square
- Scale Scenics Aluminum Micro-Mesh no. 652-3530
- Floquil Railroad Tie Brown (or equal) no. F110014
- Gap-filling CA
- Woodland Scenics, Scenic Glue no. S190

Photos of the interlocking show that for many years there was a wire mesh (perhaps chain link) fence along Front Street from just west of the Main Street crossing to the Mineola Boulevard bridge. The fence appears to be around 5 to 6 feet high and was mounted on square wooden posts. The photos show that over the years the fence was in rather poor condition and suffered from a lack of maintenance.

To duplicate the fence I cut 1/16"-square basswood stock into 8-foot lengths and weathered them. They were then temporarily taped down at 8-foot intervals. I used CA to attach Scale Scenics aluminum Micro-Mesh to the uprights. This created a realistic looking fence suitable for the scene. The mesh has a degree of stiffness that allowed me to bend it downward at intervals and create damage that matched the photos. I then weathered the mesh with a dark wash. I used the same method to secure this fence as the chain link fence.

Line poles

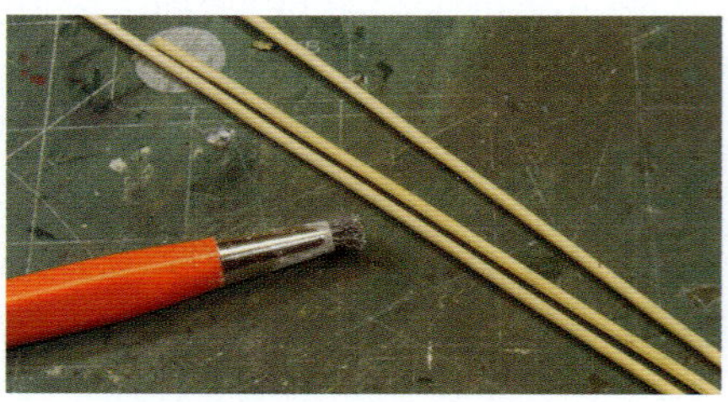

MATERIALS

- Wood dowels 1/16" and 1/8" diameter
- Basswood 1/16" for crossarms
- Basswood 1/32" x 1/16" for crossarm supports
- Floquil Railroad Tie Brown (or equal) no. F110014
- CA, thick gap-filling
- Woodland Scenics, Scenic Glue no. S190
- Crimp beads, Bead Landing (Michaels)

Photos the Nassau Interlocking complex from virtually every era show an amazing complex of poles of every size and for every purpose. Everything from short poles being used to hold up local switch and signal circuits between the tower and instrument cases, to extremely tall high-tension poles for carrying the 11,000-volt, 25-cycle traction power.

The module does not include the network of cables that crisscrossed the area. I could never get a hand in to perform any work! The poles approximate the configuration as of the mid- to late-1960s. I made most poles from 1/16" dowels.

There are several high-tension wood poles along Front Street. They carry traction power lines along the right of way. I roughed each one with a small steel wire brush to add texture to the pole. These poles are made from 1/8" dowels due to their height. I glued either half or full crossarms to the poles with CA to match photos. I used the same crimp beads from the third-rail project for insulators on the cross arms.

Vehicles and people

Automobiles and trucks were placed throughout the scene to add a sense of purpose. Keep in mind this is a very busy suburban area with considerable traffic activity. The types and ages of the vehicles should be appropriate for the time period.

The Mineola Boulevard bridge saw considerable truck traffic and was also used by several transit bus routes. The automobile commuter parking lot alongside the bridge was heavily used during the weekdays and largely empty on weekends. Front Street was also used for commuter parking along the curbs, and in the 1960s it was still a two-way street. The portion of Front Street south of the tracks was one-way to the west and commuter parking was allowed on the north side.

Main Street was and still is a busy two-way street entering the heart of the old Mineola business district. The portion to the north of the LIRR tracks was also the scene of the terminus of several trolley car lines many years ago.

Figures can also be placed throughout the scene. Commuters (in business dress) can be placed going to or from the station and their vehicles, and some being placed on the sidewalk under the Mineola Boulevard bridge. Long Island Rail Road workers can be placed going about their tasks around the tracks, third rail, and Nassau Tower, and village people can be seen going about their daily tasks such as walking along the sidewalk on the Mineola Boulevard Bridge or waiting at the Main Street crossing. As with the vehicles, figures need to match the era and the activity they are engaged in.

I made good use of my boxes of old unused figures and vehicles for this part of the build. If these parts need to be purchased there are many good examples on the new and secondary market.

CHAPTER THREE

Saving Peerless Tanning

By Lou Sassi

Rich Cobb built this HO model of Peerless Tanning for a diorama Lou built for the book *How to Build and Detail Model Railroad Scenes Volume no. 1*. Lou had Rich add freight doors so the building could be rail-served.

Cheryl Sassi holds a range pole up against the side of Peerless Tanning while her husband, Lou, photographs the building with an eye toward modeling the structure. Sometimes, you can take your own photos to model from. Choose a bright day, and check with the building owner to ensure you're not trespassing.

For about five years in the early '70s, my wife, Cheryl, and I passed the Peerless Tanning Company Mill on the corner of Briggs and Grand streets in Johnstown, N.Y., every weekday on our commute to and from work at the General Electric plant in Schenectady. Every time we drove past the old mill, I would mention to Cheryl that we should someday take photos and dimensions of it for future reference just in case I ever decided to have a miniature version built for my HO scale West Hoosic Division Railroad.

After years of contemplation, on a sunny afternoon in September 1999 we did just that. Cheryl held a range pole against the side of the building while I took photographs.

One thing I learned from reading McMartin's book (see below, right) was that the various additions and piping exiting the main structure at the right rear of the building were there to extricate the shavings from the surface of the raw hides, while the barrels and boxes in the photos contained an assortment of hides, chemicals, and coloring agents.

AND THEN IT WAS GONE I was relieved we documented Peerless when we did. In 2009 we moved from New York to North Carolina. Every year since, we would drive back upstate to visit relatives and friends in the Johnstown-Gloversville area for a few weeks in the summer, always making a point to drive down Brigg's Street and check on the old mill. (It was abandoned about the time we moved south). To our dismay, in the summer of 2012 we found an empty lot where Peerless once stood. Thanks to Cheryl and me taking the time to record it for posterity, Peerless lives on, if only in miniature.

Our visit that day sparked my interest in the manufacturing of leather and leather products. Eventually, we found a museum in Gloversville, N.Y., devoted to the history of the leather industry. While visiting the museum our host referred me to Barbara McMartin, who had written a book on the leather industry *The Glove Cities*. Peerless was mentioned a number of times in that publication, along with dozens of other mills that once flourished in the area.

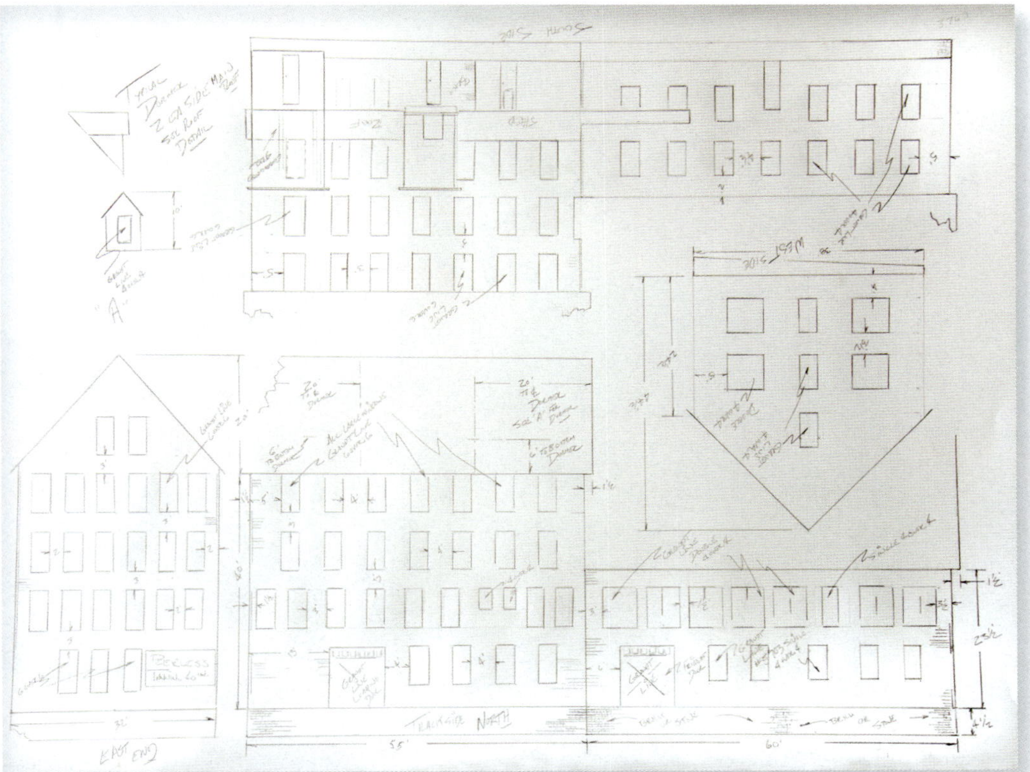

With my newfound knowledge of the business, in 2004 I decided to include Peerless in a chapter of my Kalmbach book *How to Build and Detail Model Railroad Scenes Volume no. 1* (out of print). I had my good friend Rich Cobb build an HO scale model of the building using the photos shot in 1999, along with scale drawings I made for reference. Because the real Peerless was an off-line structure, I applied a bit of artistic license to the drawings, replacing some of the windows on the north side of the building with loading doors to make it an on-line industry.

With the photos we took in '99 as a reference, I used chalks to weather the model and installed it on a 2 x 3-foot diorama. I then added a variety of barrels, pallets, boxes, and other details at the rear of the building to replicate the prototype. Finally, I laid out the streets surrounding it along with a main line track and siding on the north side of the building.

CHAPTER FOUR

This water-to-rail transfer model scene provides a lot of operating activity on Paul Dolkos' HO scale Baltimore Harbor District railroad. The photo that got Paul started (above, right) didn't have enough information to complete the scene. A photo of a similar float bridge helped Paul fill in some of the gaps. Other photos filled in more of the details.

Modeling where rails meet water

Paul J. Dolkos //

Photos by author except as noted

This view of the Wagners Point transfer bridge gives a view of the prototype but by itself it doesn't convey enough information. *Don McFall*

This photo of the float bridge on Western Maryland's Cabin Branch shows a similar operation to what Paul modeled at Wagner's Point. *George M. Leilich*

For many years, when railroads reached a wide river, lake, or other body of water, instead of building a bridge or going around it, they would often float traffic across the water on a barge or boat. And in some locations such as an island, the only way to reach a customer was via a water route.

Such railroad marine operations began early and continued to be used until the 1990s when mergers and abandonments eliminated the need for almost all of them. Today there is one traditional-style U.S. carfloat operation between New Jersey and Brooklyn in the upper New York Bay. There is also a service between Mobile, Ala., and Mexico on two large ships, each with a capacity of 115 freight cars.

For the model railroader, a carfloat operation presents the opportunity to build a unique scenery and operational feature. Prototypes operated not only along the coasts, but also on interior lakes and rivers. Because of a wide range of local conditions, the facilities to transfer railcars to and from barges and boats varied widely. They were often designed by a railroad's engineering department and built by various bridge construction companies.

The facilities consisted of two main elements. There was a float bridge—basically a ramp with track that could be raised or lowered to match the track level on the floating car carrier. While you can use a float bridge strictly as a scenic element without a barge or boat, that seems like a wasted opportunity. For that you'll want the second piece, a barge or fleet of barges that floated cars across the water. Large ferries or ships also carried rail cars, particularly on the Great Lakes and West Coast.

The scene

What is described in this chapter is an HO model of specific prototype. It is a unique design, one of a hundred or more different ones in the U.S. and Canada. Even if the design doesn't match up with your taste or prototype, you may find some helpful points of interest.

The operation described and pictured here of the tug *Hawkins Point* shepherding Western Maryland barge 14 at Wagners Point with the Royster Fertilizer plant and Baltimore industryscape in the background was one of several remote marine terminals served by the Western Maryland out of its Port Covington yard in Baltimore, Md. At Wagners Point the WM joined forces with the Pennsylvania Railroad in 1916 at the request of industries south of downtown to provide competitive rail service against the Baltimore & Ohio. The area is surrounded on three sides by water and was the only access available to the B&O's competitors.

Building the float bridge

The float bridge ramp at Wagners Point was raised and lowered with a hand-operated chain and cable hoist to match the height of the floating barge. Other float bridge designs floated on pontoons that were either filled with water or drained to match the height of the barge sitting in water. Very busy rail-marine transfer operations employed heavy-duty electric-powered cable and sheave arrangements to raise and lower the bridges.

The first phase of my modeling project was to establish the details of design and overall size of the float bridge. I had just two photos of the Wagners Point bridge but no plans or drawings. So I roughed out some sketches focusing on appropriate clearances for the rolling stock moving on and off the barge. The resulting measurements are listed in the photos. Early on I would also suggest gathering the detail parts before starting construction per the list.

1. The float bridge is built mainly using styrene strips and shapes. The key pieces constructed first are three girder frames that provided the prototype's strength. To maintain a uniform size and shape of the frames, I constructed a simple jig on a piece of scrap lumber to maintain uniformity. The small laced black girders in the photos on the sloping outer edges are from Central Valley Model Works heavy-duty laced box girders package. The black piece at the base is a scale 24 x 30-inch beam from the CV girder set. The white sections are Evergreen I-beams that match the width of the CV pieces. Extra details were added from Evergreen styrene strip stock to match photos.

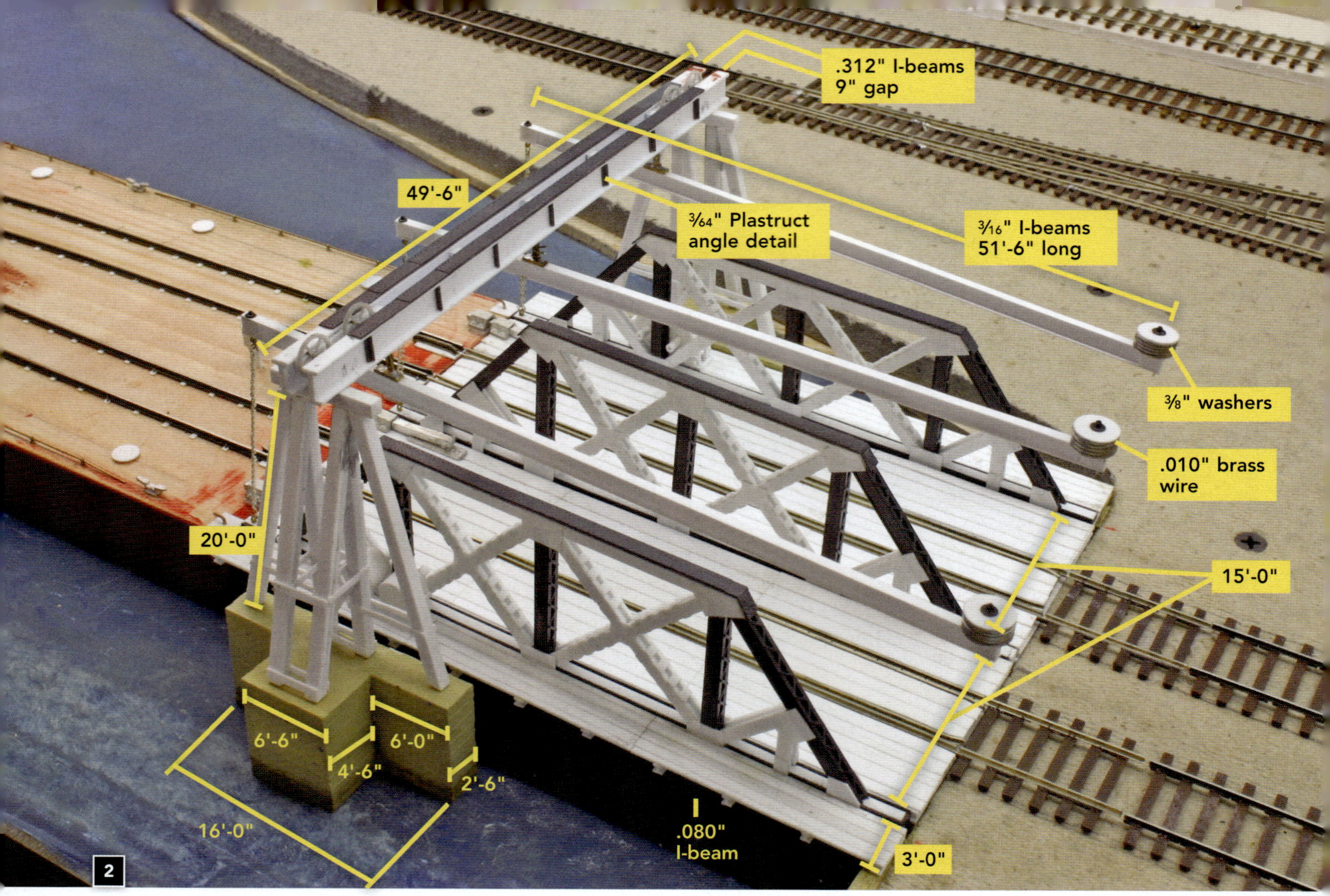

2. With the trusses complete, it's time to work on the float bridge assembly. This photo shows how the parts fit together.

The length of top beam, two .312" I-beams set with a scale 9" gap between them to accommodate pulleys, is a scale 49'-6" long. On the webs of the beams I placed 3⁄64" Plastruct angle detail.

The counterweight beams are made from three 3⁄16" I-beams, 51'-6" long. They hang from the top beam with two flat brass strips pinned so they can move. There is a stack of five 3⁄8" washers as counterweights to keep front chains taut.

The distance between bridge trusses is 15 feet, and the width of entire float bridge floor 41 feet, including the 3-foot width of outside walkways. The walkways are supported by pieces of .080" I beam bracing.

I used three pieces of .010" brass wire to simulate the cables that positioned the front edge height up or down with barge.

For the bridge floor base, I cut two pieces of .060-inch styrene sheet a scale 15 feet wide and 50.6 feet long. These fit between the girder frames. The rail on my float bridge is code 55 Micro Engineering flextrack matching much of the track in the Wagners Point yard. I glued the track with the ties on to the styrene floor base with about 2" of track hanging out on the land side. This simplified soldering power feeders outside the bridge. I built the floor level up to rail height or just below it with styrene representing 12"-wide planking.

I then added planking on the two outside bridge girders, creating 3-foot-wide outside walkways. In the photo you can see some bracing underneath. This completes the basic bridge floor. Next is the construction of the supports for the chains that raise and lower the floor to match the changing rail height on the barge due to tide and load.

3. There are three major pieces that make up the hoisting system: concrete base piers for the uprights, the vertical supports, and the heavy cross beam. I made a mold to cast the piers. It consists of wall pieces that form the outside shape of the pier. Each pier measures 8 scale feet high, 6'-6" square in the front, 9 feet wide x 2 feet deep in the back.

The mold can be built using stripwood or styrene strips. Slight openings between its board pieces in the mold create ridges found on prototypes. Build the mold so when the plaster has set some of the wall sections can be pulled away horizontally from the pier molding. I find plaster molding easy, quick, and satisfying.

The upright supports on the top of the two piers carry the double I-beams, providing a 20 foot clearance underneath. Each support is built up with six scale 12"-square styrene pieces. If desired, wood grain could be simulated on the timbers using course sandpaper.

The two double I-beams on the supports are 49 feet long with spacers between them, creating a scale 9" gap between to accept pulleys for cabling. No cabling is visible in the prototype photo, so none was modeled. Vertical 3⁄64" angles are glued in on the beam webs per the prototype. On the beams' top edges, .010" styrene strips are applied to represent additional strengthening.

Hanging from the two cross beams are three scale 51'-6" long beams with chain and cables hanging down to the bridge platform to raise or lower the platform to conform with the barge height. The lower

3

beams pivot on overlapping small flat pieces pinned together. On the water side there is a chain hooked to the ends of the three beams and the bridge deck below. At the other end there are weights (five stacked washers) that keep the chains in the front taut. Dropping down from the weights is a .010" brass wire representing a cable. There is a small diameter piece of tubing, strictly cosmetic, in the ground that the cable drops into.

The one last detail on the bridge to model are two pairs of round containers that I presume cover cable spools. These have a wheel for reeling the cable in or out to raise or lower the bridge.

Building the barge

Details on the barge deck show in this April 8,1972, view, including the small crew cabin for trips in inclement weather. *Charles Kilbourne*

The end view reveals the unusual rail positioning, possibly to shift weight to the barge center, although this has not been confirmed. *Charles Kilbourne*

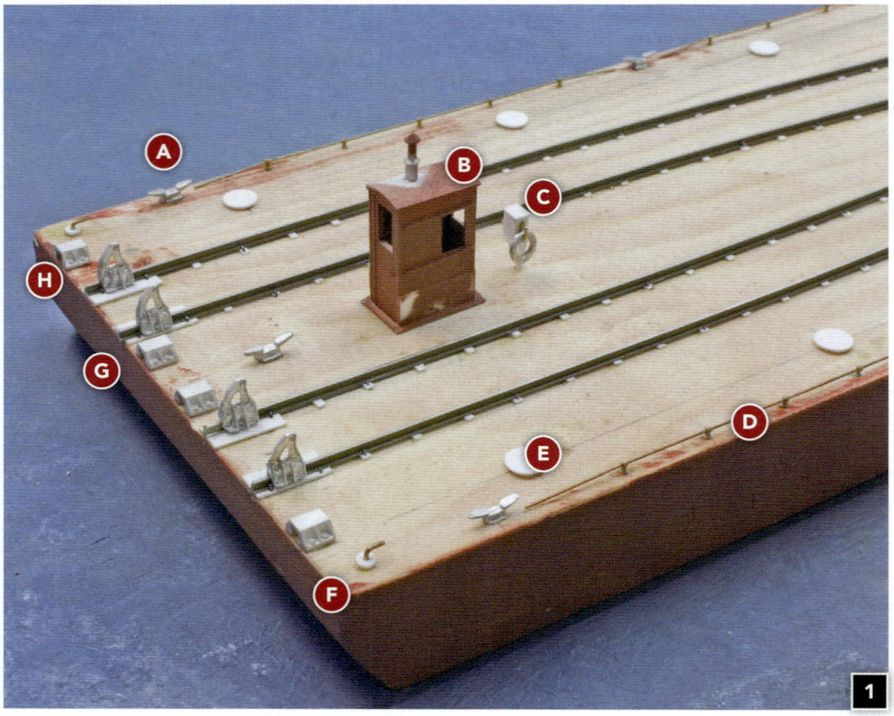

1

BARGE PARTS

A. ⅜" or similar cast cleat
B. Scratchbuilt cabin with styrene and cast stack.
C. Bill box on post with life preserver hanging on hook
D. Low railing running through low stanchions.
E. Hatch covers, 18" punched paper circle
F. Corner bridge hook, wire or Frenchman River Model Works
G. Buda wheel stop, Custom Finishing Models
H. Toggle bar pockets, on both ends of barge. Toggle bars are on water end

2

1. Now you can turn your attention to modeling a barge, a far less complicated task. The eight-car barge I modeled is a scale 194 feet long, 36 feet wide, and sits 7 feet above the waterline. That barge height matched up with my float bridge rails. It could be varied, particularly a bit lower if necessary. Longer railroad barges had greater car capacity. The Western Maryland had 210-foot-long barges that could carry up to 10 cars and 345-footers that provided space for 22 cars.

My barge body is a length of 1x6 clear white pine cut to size. To create a barge with a deck 7 feet above water, I glued ¼"-thick wood strips around the bottom edges to increase the thickness of the hull. I rounded the corners with a file. Once I was satisfied with the shape, I filled any crevices with Bondo autobody putty. I painted the hull and sanded it and repeated the work until the surfaces would pass for steel. The process went quickly.

Next, I drew lines for rail placement on the barge. Be sure they match with the track spacing on the float bridge. The prototype WM centers were 14'-10"—mine are 15 feet. On WM's smaller two-track barges the track spacings were narrowed to 11 feet in the center. I assume this was to shift some weight to the center, but I've

PARTS LIST

Nautical cast items are available from Sea Port Model Works, Frenchman River Model Works, and Bluejacket Ship Crafters. These companies have several options to fit your needs.

Cleats: 14⅜" long, 6 each side, 1 each end centered
Bridge hook, 1 each corner
Toggle pockets: 4 each end, 4 on float bridge
Toggle bars: 4 on float bridge
Life preserver: mount on post or cabin each end
Handrail stanchions for low railing along barge edge
Custom Finishing Models
Buda Wheel Stops: 4 on non-loading end
Proto87: stores
Rail chairs: tie plate under rails

been unable to confirm this.

I used code 55 rail, but the prototype listed 90-pound rail in its specs, so code 83 would follow the prototype. Under the rails I used .015" styrene for what are called rail chairs in WM prototype documentation. Doing it again I would use Proto87 etched tie plates and its small spikes. Since the General Electric 44-ton locomotive runs on to the float to switch cars, power feeders are required and come up under the barge.

There a number of other details to be added to the barge deck. Refer to the photos for the placement. The small cabin on the barge measures 5'-0" long, 2'-6" wide, and 7'-4" high. I built mine with styrene. The hatch covers on the barge are for access into nine hull compartments.

2. The barge lettering is from white decals printed on a modeling friend's Alps machine. I created the master with the purchase of Western Maryland letter set from www.railfonts.com.

Bringing it together

I placed the elements of the float installation to verify positioning of all elements.

The Wagner's Point float bridge docking area had one long as well as a short wooden pier that made it easy for workers to walk along beside the barge's length. The short dock side made it easy for a tug to push the float into place. Many other terminal float areas had more open water to dock a barge. My flanking piers are built with stripwood. Including a tug in the scene is not mandatory, but the addition is hard to resist. Mine is a Walthers tug kit.

The water surface is a stippled with varied colors; blue, gray, white and brown. If you're not satisfied with the appearance, simply dab more of the desired color on the model water surface. Once you like the color range, coat the surface with a gloss clear medium. The gloss gives the surface a wet look. With heavy applications in some spots you can create some low waves. I used Golden Artist Colors Regular Gel Gloss.

The barge could be moved to a different location if such moves were desired. But I only have the one barge terminal and I would be afraid having cars roll off the barge during transit. While not glued or otherwise fastened into position, its positioning is relatively stable due to the slight tackiness of the gloss medium.

So I'm satisfied leaving it where it is and letting the single position serve as a small staging yard. I may not even change out rolling stock between operating sessions. Nobody remembers what box or tank cars were there before. Its also easy enough to change out equipment as desired. That's my choice.

CHAPTER FIVE

Modeling an old station

Alex Belida // Photos by author except as noted

In its heyday, the Woodsboro station was the main shipping point for goldfish. That business thrived in the early 1900s when fish from area ponds were taken to the station for distribution all over the United States. Experts say lime in the soil and water gave the fish a much-desired intense golden hue.

WHAT'S IN THE PHOTO

Model

1. Mt. Albert board-and-batten siding
2. Tichy Train Group windows and doors
3. Northeastern Scale Lumber standing-seam metal roofing
3. Scale Structures Ltd. train-order signal
4. Postal Telegraph and Commercial Cable sign from online images
5. Milk cans standing in for goldfish cans
6. Platform lantern

Prototype

1. These canisters are shipping containers for goldfish.
2. Signs on the depot entry show it was serviced by Adams Express and used by Postal Telegraph and Commercial Cable.
3. Train order signal. For years, the station was staffed by an agent who received train orders. But after 1949 orders were received at the station by the train conductor using a handset to speak directly to the dispatcher. The only person to actually use the station then was a traveling clerk who checked local accounts and left waybills in the phone box for the conductor.
4. Pennsylvania Railroad (ex-Frederick & Pennsylvania Line) tracks to Frederick, Md.
5. Platform lantern
6. Old Creagerstown Road

The train station on Old Creagerstown Road in Woodsboro, Md., was built in 1883 and served as an active passenger stop until 1948. Trains were first operated by the Frederick & Pennsylvania Line and the route was later taken over by the Pennsylvania Railroad (PRR). The segment of the railway running through Woodsboro and other PRR properties in the area were sold to the State of Maryland in 1982. The state later sold about 20 miles of the branch to the Maryland Midland Railway. The track that runs past Woodsboro Station is still in place. Although no trains pass by, the same track farther on is used by the Midland to service a nearby quarry.

Unfortunately, the station fell into disrepair after it stopped being an active stop. It has now been restored by the Woodsboro Historical Society, which currently uses the interior space to store both railroad and non-railroad memorabilia.

I discovered Woodsboro station and decided to model it in HO after my son Brian and his family bought a house 100 yards away. The historical society provided archival photos and gave me permission to use them along with a plan of the depot with floor dimensions.

The building was 10 feet wide by 45 feet long with a bay-type window sticking out in the passenger ticketing section. The adjacent baggage-freight portion was 10 feet wide by 16 feet long.

1

I used Mt. Albert board-and-batten siding for the superstructure. The corners are braced with 1/8"-square stripwood.

2

I used Tichy train Group styrene windows and doors I matched to my photographs.

3

I cut a piece of sheet styrene, scribed, as a base for the station platform supported by ¼" stripwood beams. I also installed a wall with a doorway inside the station to separate the freight area from the passenger office side, as in the original.

4

I stained the wood (both sides) with a brown shoe polish and alcohol mix. I then painted the structure with white primer and the window and door parts Tamiya Flat Brown (XF-10). After sanding the exterior of the building, I painted it with Tamiya Buff (XF-57). I then cut styrene corner angles and painted them Flat Brown. I painted the base strip of wood around the structure to match.

5

I built a frame to support the prototype's standing-seam metal roof, building it in such a way that the roof can be removed to view the interior detailing. I used Northeastern Scale Lumber standing seam metal roofing to simulate what was used in the restored station.

6

I framed the windows and doors inside the structure and painted them Buff. I installed the glazing in the windows and doors and installed them in the building.

7

I used a piece of Sculptamold I had previously cast and cut it to resemble the shape of the stone stairway and landing leading to the side entrance to the restored station. I then carved the Sculptamold to create steps and to reflect the stone pattern. I painted it with a brown earth tone and gave it an India Ink wash.

8

I made signs to duplicate those on the station. The metal scroll work on the Post and Cable sign, which hung out from the wall, came from a lamp post in my scrapbox.

9

Next I attached gooseneck lamps over the side and freight doors plus an overhead light inside the passenger area and another in the freight area, all Evans Designs pico light-emitting diodes (LEDs). These are powered by a 3V battery hidden under the station platform. The on-off switch is concealed amongst bushes along the back wall.

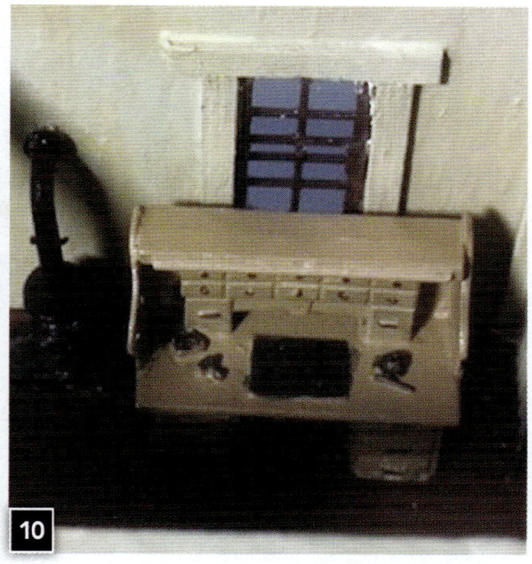

10

I added a Scale Structures potbelly stove inside the station, connected to the chimney on the back wall. I also added a rolltop desk with swivel chair.

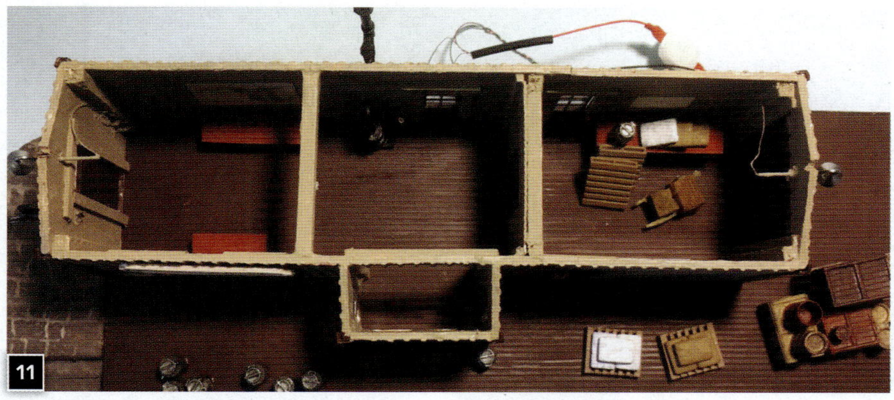

11

I scratchbuilt two benches to go inside the passenger section and a storage shelf on the freight side. I added Tichy shutters on some windows in front. A passenger bench, fish cans (milk cans), and assorted cargo including mail bags were added on the platform.

12

I built and painted a train order semaphore signal from Scale Structures Ltd. and placed it on the entry steps. The old photo shows wooden steps, not the stone of the renovated station.

13

The final touch was the lantern on a post on the platform. I used the clear "glass" insert from a Utah Pacific illuminated lantern with an Evans pico LED inside, all mounted on brass tubing.

MATERIALS LIST

- Mt. Albert SS-BB-HO-12-4x12 board and batten siding
- Stripwood, various sizes
- Scrap wire
- Sheet styrene and styrene corner angles
- Tichy windows and doors and glazing
- Tamiya Flat Brown and Buff paint and Model Color Cavalry Brown and Model Master Rust, Black, and Wood, plus red and yellow acrylic
- Gesso white primer
- Formula 560 Canopy Glue
- Loctite super glue
- Brown shoe polish and alcohol mix, india ink mix (stain)
- Northeastern Scale Lumber 55061 ribbed metal roofing
- Evans Designs 3V Battery Powered LEDs: 2 gooseneck and 1 nano and 2 pico
- Scale Structures Ltd. potbelly stove and chimney, bench, rolltop desk and swivel chair, train-order signal semaphore
- Rusty Stumps crates, sacks, and pallets
- Brass tubing (1.57mm x .355mm)
- Utah Pacific illuminated lantern

CHAPTER SIX

Backdrops bring a snowy scene to life

Mark Dance // Photos by the author

This photo by Theresa Smith shows Farron, B.C., in the early 1950s, when her father worked for the Canadian Pacific. It and articles by Mike Dannemann inspired Mark Dance to add a snow scene to his model railroad. *Theresa Smith*

Mark had to take a few liberties with the prototype to get the scene to fit on his N scale Canadian Pacific Columbia & Western Ry. layout, but the final scene is recognizably Farron, British Columbia.

My N scale Columbia & Western Ry. is a re-creation of the Canadian Pacific's Boundary, Slocan, and Kaslo subdivisions in the mountainous southeastern corner of British Columbia. The layout's name is taken from the original 1890s charter under which rails were boldly pushed westward through the beautiful but challenging terrain.

At the highest point on the Boundary subdivision was Farron, a helper station that for more than 50 years was responsible for the care and feeding of the numerous pusher locomotives stationed there. Regardless of the time of year, pushers would be summoned down from Farron to meet trains of either direction. They would trundle down 25 miles to the eastern or western foot of the grades and then couple up to help raise the trains up 2,500 feet of elevation. Again and again man and machine would repeat this dance, braving not only technical challenges measured in tons, miles and horsepower on the 2.2 percent grades, but also natural challenges measured in degrees Celcius and feet of snowfall. It was partly as homage to these railroaders that I sought to re-create this helper operation into the C&W's operating plan as I designed the layout. I toyed with the idea of building Farron as a snow scene, but was cautioned against this by experienced modelers who had struggled with the reliability problems plaster snow can create around trackwork.

Two things settled my mind to pursue modeling Farron in full-on winter. The first was finding a photograph of Farron by Theresa Smith, taken during the early 1950s when her father worked for the CPR and Theresa, her family, and a dozen more families called isolated Farron home. The second was a series of articles by noted Denver & Rio Grande Western modeler Mike Danneman on how to create dramatic, heavy snow scenes using a combination of Hydrocal plaster for ground snow and, more importantly, marble dust around the delicate trackwork. Ignoring that Mike is an accomplished artist in addition to his impressive modeling skills, if he could make it work surely I could too? What follows, starting with the backdrops, is how I created a reliable snow scene evocative of Ms. Smith's moody photo using techniques anyone can master ... honest!

Painting a snowy mountain backdrop

Painting a snowy backdrop is a matter of following some easy steps:

1. Choose your paint. The backdrops behind nearly all the Columbia & Western are dominated by two things, sky and trees, so I have pint-sized cans of inexpensive latex blue and green wall paint that I use everywhere for consistency. The blue was matched to published photos of notable scenes and the green was matched to the model evergreens I use the most: bulk Heki and Woodland Scenics models. A mixture of these paints creates a gray base color. Into this base I mix in Titanium White and Mars Black tube acrylic paints, lightening the base for distant hills and snow cover and darkening the mix as I paint closer scenes and create the dark shadows between the boughs in the foreground tree line.

2. Establish the horizon and the landform profiles you will paint. I use a very light pencil line made right on the backdrop for these guide lines, drawing them as an observer would see them from the their perspective in the aisle. For example, consider if a trackside observer is looking "up" at surrounding ridgelines above the tracks and therefore the painted backdrop should end with a simple ridge-top treeline against the sky, or would an observer's perspective be higher, allowing them to see over adjacent ridges to distant peaks or even up valleys (as shown at right)?

3. Break the painting down into 3 "zones." From back to front, in the order you paint them, they are: a) sky; b) any background scenery visible beyond the immediate tree line perhaps comprising up to five sub-zones; and c) a foreground tree line immediately adjacent to the modeled scenery. I found it helpful to paint each of these three zones in a different manner.

PAINTING THE DISTANT SKY

No magic here, just the conventional approach of gently blending from a basic sky color at the top of the backdrop down to white at the distant horizon.

I wanted an ominous sky above Farron to leave the impression of snowstorms on the way, so my basic sky color here is quite gray mixed from white, muddied with a bit of sky blue, and the smallest trace of Mars black. If I had wanted to impart a cheery, sun-drenched mood, I would have used just the sky blue I use in other areas of the layout.

Either way I blend down to pure white at the horizon by running a wet roller horizontally back and forth on the backdrop, ensuring that the color transition is smooth with no visible discontinuities. Add clouds per your favorite technique.

PAINTING THE BACKGROUND SCENERY (IF VISIBLE):

If background scenery will be visible behind the foreground tree line, paint it in next working from distant mountain peaks forward. I break up the background scenery into four or five sub-zones, each comprising scenery layers approximately the same distance from the viewer with each sub-zone getting progressively closer.

All parts of a sub-zone will have the same starting color of a hue that represents the shadowy areas of the forest in the sub-zone. These shadow colors are mixed by adding consecutively more sky blue and tree green to your horizon sky color to darken the starting color of each sub-zone as they approach the viewer.

I try to paint and finish each sub-zone completely before moving on to the next-closer sub-zone because I like working with wet paint as the highlights blend together better, and so I can build up colors in a sub-zone from the same mix of staring shadow paint without having to re-create the exact tone later.

Here comes the fun part: the ridge lines and separating valleys. I add a touch of titanium white to the shadow color (titanium white being more opaque then zinc white) and, following the previously sketched pencil lines, I paint the sub-zone downward from the ridgelines, stopping before reaching the bottom of the valleys. Add a touch more white and repeat the process stopping a bit shorter in the valleys then you did last time. Continue this process until you are applying pure white "snow" to just the tops and shoulders of the ridgelines and the peaks of the distant mountains.

Move to the next sub-zone and start by adding a bit more tree green and sky blue to the previous shadow color to create a darker-hued shadow color for this sub-zone. Repeat the highlighting by adding white paint to the shadow color and highlighting the ridge lines until you are adding pure white to just the tops of scenic features.

A note on details. As the sub-zones you are painting move closer to the observer, details of the trees will become larger and easier to distinguish. You can quickly simulate this with your brushstroke. For example, for the most distant ridgelines and mountain tops where individually trees cannot be distinguished, I will brush horizontally in long, uninterrupted strokes. As I turn to paint closer sub-zones I switch to vertical strokes allowing the brushes bristles to re-create the spiky tops of trees in a treeline. Closer still and individual vertical strokes can be used to imply individual trees and then, yet closer, tree branches.

Helpful hints for painting the foreground tree line:

Keep a snowed model tree (of the type and size you intend to plant against the backdrop) handy as a reference while you paint the adjacent treeline. It will help remind you of the size, shape and color of the model trees you are trying to match.

Before you paint the trees, get their attitude right (make sure they're vertical)! Use a dark shade of your green/blue/black mix to sketch vertical lines for the trunks of the foreground treeline trees first. This will help establish proper size, spacing and inclination of the foreground trees. You can come back to fill their branches out and add snow to them as second and third steps.

A small spirit level held up to the backdrop is useful in assuring your painted trees remain plumb.

Snow ground cover

Large areas of drift snow are easily and quickly built up using Mike Danneman's sifted Hydrocal technique. Like Mike, I used Woodland Scenics Lightweight Hydrocal, which is very white and dries smooth and hard if thoroughly wetted. I load up a small tea strainer with the Hydrocal and tap on the strainer, applying Hydrocal right over the wetted Sculptamold I use for basic landforms.

I spray the sifted Hydrocal so it is thoroughly wetted to the point of running like a liquid and has a smooth, wet surface everywhere without a hint of powder. It takes a bit of practice to build up the necessary judgment to know when to stop spraying. Yes, you will over-wet the plaster occasionally, but sprinkling on more plaster helps to absorb the excess water. Still "forewarned is forearmed," so make sure you cover every surface the flowing Hydrocal may run onto.

My experience is that there are two keys to this process. The first is using a spray bottle that very finely atomizes the water into a mist so water drops are so small they don't disturb the Hydrocal. After quite a search I found a refillable cologne bottle at the perfume counter of a local drug store. The second key is very strong index fingers as it takes a lot of pumps to distribute all the water this process requires! Oh, and because of all the water used in the process, I have learned (the hard way) to add a drop of disinfectant to the Hydrocal to inhibit mold in my snow!

The good news is you can cover a lot of layout with snow fast this way and the same technique works on structures, trees, and lineside details, so it is well worth mastering.

Snowed tracks

Perhaps the biggest challenge that concerned me about deep snow scenes was modelling the snow on the roadbed so deep that just the tops of the railheads mark where the trains tread. I worry about adding anything in and around proven, operating trackwork, and the thought of embedding all the rails in the 20-foot-long Farron scene in plaster was concerning to say the least and in reality almost a showstopper. Mike Danneman's use of marble dust to effectively ballast the tracks in a heavy, rock "snow" gave me some comfort, but with no personal experience with the material I still feared surprises. In an attempt to plan for the unknown while I was designing the layout, I thought hard about how I could reach every nook and cranny of the trackwork in case remediation was needed and elected to make the roadbed for the whole Farron scene removable complete with track, switch machines and wiring so its track and wiring could be tested independently of the layout. As it turned out, that decision saved my bacon!

I bought several bags of Arizona Rock & Mineral marble dust snow that in the bag was pristine white with a touch of sparkle. Perfect! With Farron removed from the layout and laying on the floor of the layout room in temporary foam cradles all the track was within easy reach. I poured the marble dust liberally between and outside the rails save around the switch frogs and points.

A flanger blade profile sanded into one side of a short length of styrene box tubing served well as a home-made flanger. Another short length of styrene glued perpendicular to the blade served as a handle, and I was in business. Sweeping the tracks a few times created the flangeways and snow profile I desired.

Then came the isopropyl alcohol wetting agent, followed by several applications of dilute matte medium (decanted to remove any chalk). As it is real rock, the marble dust stayed in place nicely including holding the flangeway gaps cut by the styrene plow.

The nasty surprise was apparent when everything had dried and the marble dust was no longer the pristine white snow but had dried more the color of beach sand! Yikes! Mike had noted there might be some yellowing but this was far more than I expected.

Mike also provided the solution: gesso, a white paint mixture artists apply to surfaces to prepare them for painting. Painting over *all* the yellowed marble dust did do the trick, though it required five nail-biting, pain-staking applications! Now this discoloration may not happen to everyone's marble dust, but again, forewarned is forearmed so plan ahead and consider how you would address yellowing snow around your delicate trackwork, you know, just in case.

- I can get exactly the structure I want, especially the doors and windows where the selection is sparse in N scale
- I can work with a variety of skilled tradespeople who have put in the investment and know how to get the best results from their various equipment so they can consistently cut window mullions down to .010" (1.5 N scale inches!)
- I have built up a library of elements which can be easily modified for new projects
- Assembling a double-hung window from up to five separate adhesive-backed layers is fast and allows me to paint frames and mullions/muntins separately to assure perfect color separation
- All my buildings are now built around a central laserboard skeleton of slot and tab construction, which assures stiffness, accuracy, and perpendicularity as well as providing interior walls to block views and constrain light spread from internal LEDs.
- I can design my own ultra thin (N Scale ½" thick) shingles that lay down straight every time. Their secret is a tear-away stiffener strip along the top edge!

Buildings

While there are a few commercial models amongst the Farron structures (the enclosed water tank is an old CS Models kit and the bunkhouse, speeder shed, and privy are single-piece resin castings from my friend Geoff Gooderham) the majority are custom "laser-scratchbuilt" buildings of my own design.

At Farron this includes a couple of CPR Type 2 section houses, the portable depot, and several standard tool sheds. I design the building in a 2D CAD drafting package—frequently using prototype plans—with custom windows, doors, walls and stairways each from multiple layers of laserboard, but then send the file to a commercial shop for cutting. I have really come to enjoy building structures this way for a number of reasons:

When it comes to adding snow to the building roofs, Mike suggested trowling on artist's modelling paste with a palette knife and I did this on the water tank. While the modeling paste is a bright white and dries nice and hard, I had difficulty creating a smooth surface on a moderate sized roof with it. The paste also tended to lay on a bit thicker than I wished.

After the initial experiments I reverted to the tried and true: sifted and sprayed lightweight Hydrocal. The gently falling plaster pleasingly catches window casements and rafter ends and other details piling up naturally on stair treads and railings: much better! The only tricks using the sifted plaster involve protecting the structure from all the water this approach uses, for which plastic wrap comes in handy, and minimizing handling of the snowed building lest the dry snow realistically flake and slide off in a sheet on unsuspecting model people below.

How to add heavy snow to coniferous trees

At 3,200 feet elevation, the forests of the Monashee Mountains are covered with (adopting best Carl Sagan voice) "billions and billions" of coniferous trees. While narrow benchwork can help reduce the number of trees your model will eventually need, you are still likely to require many hundred. I estimate that in the 40 square foot area of the Farron scene there are 2,000 to 2,500 N scale trees.

The good news is this tree density is probably ½ to ⅓ of what I use in the non-snowed areas of the layout because the visual density of snowed trees allows them to be spread out more. The not so good news is that's still a lot of trees, but if you want an impressively deep forest and at some point you have to pay the piper.

I chose to buy rather than twist my own bottlebrush trees and purchased many, many boxes of the unflocked Heki evergreens in sizes up to 6" tall, which are a decently impressive height in N scale. Unflocked, the shiny plastic "branches" of these trees leave something to be desired, but with snow on them they are fine for me, especially in large forest groupings.

Snowing the conifers is straightforward if a bit tedious: using an awl I punched a grid of holes on 2" centers into a sheet of extruded-foam insulation board, enough holes to hold about 100 trees at a time spaced far enough apart that I can get the atomizer between the trees. I then add snow and water to each tree in the same manner as I described for creating snow drift ground cover, wetting the sifted lighweight Hydrocal until it is just on the verge of running before moving on to the next tree. By the time I have made a pass through the batch, the first trees are fully dry and ready for the next snow layer. I find three or four passes adequate for heavy, bough-breaking coverage. Once dry, use the awl to punch a hole in the snow ground cover, grip the base of the tree with needle-nosed pliers and plant it with a drop of white glue. The tree's hardened plaster snow is reasonably robust, but will flake off if handled, so plant the trees away from where hands and arms will be during operations and maintenance.

CHAPTER SEVEN

Pop-up railcar scrapping

M.R. Snell // Photos by the author

A Walthers HO scale Airslide covered hopper is the centerpiece of the railcar scrapping scene. M.R. Snell used two of the models to get all of the parts he needed for his model.

M.R. Snell encountered the scrapping scene one day along an unused track outside a local CSX yard where a crew was busy reducing an Airslide hopper into nothing more than steel panels and parts. He took a few photos for reference, then got to work on his model.

Modern railroading is a constantly changing landscape. Locomotives are more powerful, commodities are changing, and railcar design is constantly evolving, partly due to industry changes and also due to rules on the lifespan of interchange equipment.

Many of the railcars we've become accustomed to seeing are being retired and scrapped due to their ages, and often it's no longer large scrap operations doing the cutting. For those modeling the modern era, this can present both modeling and traffic opportunities as many older cars are now scrapped by smaller "pop-up" scrap operations utilizing nothing more than unused team or yard tracks where cars are cut up and removed, either by truck or gondola. This was the situation I encountered one day along an unused track outside a local CSX yard where a crew was busy reducing an Airslide hopper into nothing more than steel panels and parts.

Railcar scrapping has always been a largely underground part of the rail industry. Age, damage and traffic changes can all lead to the demise of a railcar and dismantling is done by contractors both large and small. After watching this operation over several days I realized it would be ideal for a model railroad since it uses a bare minimum of real estate, it's an easy scene to build, and it offers a variety of traffic including any carbody type as an inbound load and possibly gondolas full of scrap as outbound loads.

WHAT'S IN THE PHOTO

Model

1. Worker with welding torch—Woodland Scenics

2. Flopped open hatches—Walthers Airslide parts with Plastruct tubing collars on roof

3. Interior of car painted to match prototype photo

4. Plano roofwalk

Prototype

1. Pickup with utility body

2. Worker with welding torch

3. Hatch flopped open

4. Visible interior of hopper

5. Rust at top of interior compartment that never touched the lading

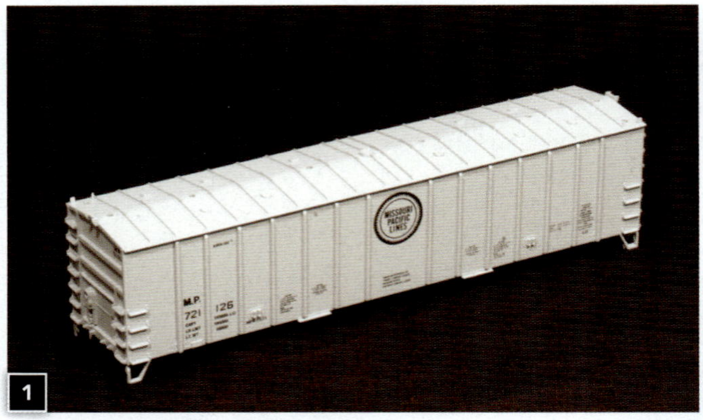

1

Since every project begins with a choice of models, in this instance I found a Walthers Airslide hopper that would be excellent for representing the car in the prototype photo. Although not as detailed as some later models, the Walthers model features a one-piece molded shell with separate underbody, making it easy to work with whether using a kit or ready-to-run model as the starting point. For this project I used two kits, one for the feature model and the second to contribute parts and scene details.

2

Before starting this project we'll need to first understand the process of scrapping the car in the prototype photo. Prior to breaking out the torch, the scrapper has laid the car on its side without its trucks. This places the car onto a solid surface and also makes access to the rooftop and underframe easier for the crew. The next step was to remove the roof in two sections, which is the point of the operation I chose to model, with one half removed and on the ground while the second half still remains on the car.

To begin, I located the center of the roof lengthwise, easily identified by the extra rib across the roof, then marked the spot.

3

Using a no. 11 blade held at a slight angle toward the roof, I repeatedly scored the joint between roof and car side from the center point to the end of the car, cutting deeper with each pass until the score was about halfway through the thick car sides.

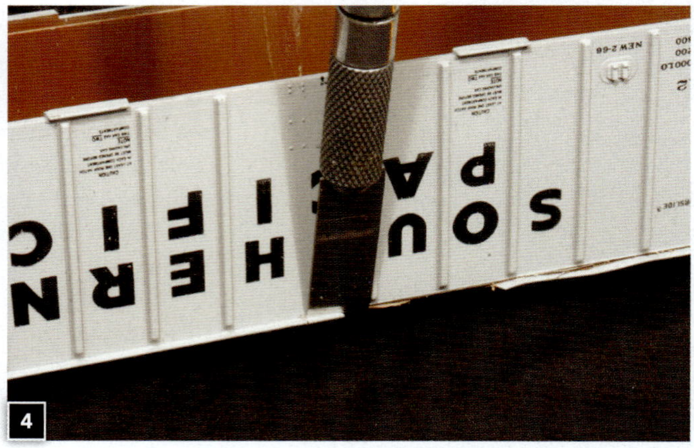

4

Next, I turned the shell upside down and used a no. 17 chisel blade to cut through the roof overhang, cutting it flush with the car sides.

5

Now this roof section could be removed, either whole or piecemeal. I found it easier to remove the roof in multiple sections by using a motor tool cutoff attachment; cutting the roof back approximately 3/16" from each side as well as the end and center to ensure I did not damage them.

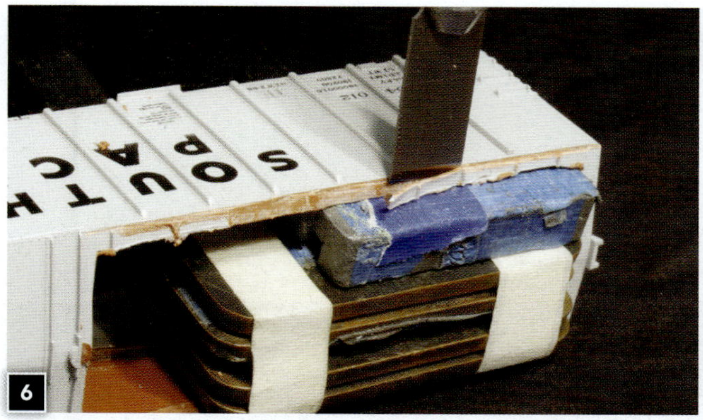

6

With the bulk of the roof panels cut away, I next laid the car on its side and built up a support for the side walls so the plastic would not snap under the pressure of knife application. Now I used a no. 18 chisel blade to cut the remaining roof sections away, placing the blade in the scores made along the roof seam and cutting downward through the seam, leaving a straight cut along the length of the seam.

7

Finally I used a file to smooth out the interior sides and roof seam edge.

8

I removed the roofwalk support from the end of the car and was left with a car with only half a roof, similar to the car in the prototype photo.

OPENING THE HATCH

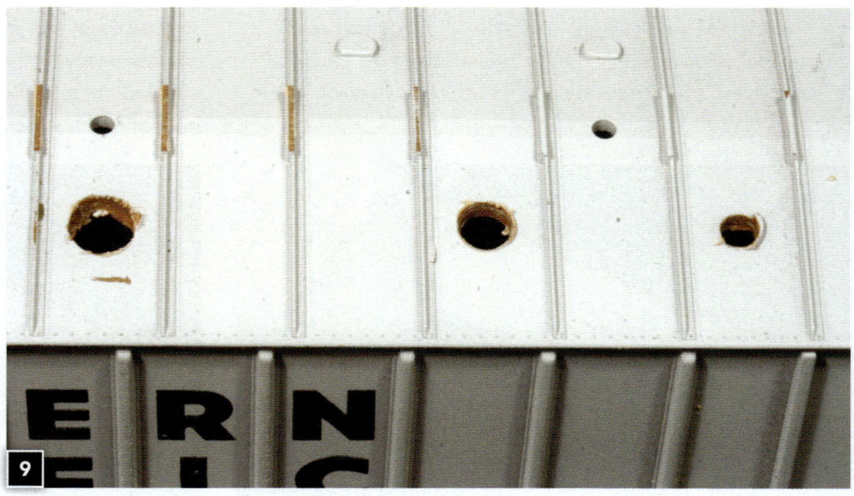

9

Now that the biggest modification had been completed, I turned to one smaller but equally important task from a visual perspective—the open roof hatches. As the car was laid down, several roof hatches fell open as their hinges were on the low side of the roof. Typical of many kits, the Walthers model features mounting studs to hold the hatch castings and these would need to be replaced with holes in the roof.

To accomplish this, I drilled a series of progressively larger holes in each location to be opened up, starting with a small hole to act as a guide for the larger bits. Once I had drilled the guide hole into each stud using a $1/16$" drill held in a pin vise, I then drilled a second hole into the first using a $1/8$" bit. To prevent damaging the areas of the roof around the hatches, I used an extremely slow speed and every time the bit would grab, I reversed the drill and allowed several rotations of the drill before continuing forward. Finally I followed this with a $1/4$" drill bit, opening the holes to the correct size, then trimmed away any leftover remnants using a no. 11 blade.

10

With the holes for the roof hatches complete, I now had to add collars around each hatch. Standard around any rooftop application, a collar prevents rainwater running along the roof from entering the hole by raising the hatch opening above the surface of the roof. While this may look difficult, it required nothing more than cutting three 1/16"-high collars from a length of Plastruct no. 90606 ¼-inch tubing cemented to the roof using Zap+, a cyanoacrylate adhesive (CA) with a gap filler. I then sanded across the top of the three collars using a medium emery board that would simultaneously contact all of them, enabling me to easily ensure they were all the same height.

11

Now that the hatch openings were complete I focused on the hatches themselves. Separate components from the roof, the hatches feature the collars molded into the underside of each casting. Soon a little careful work with a no. 18 blade had cut through the collar leaving only the flat underside of the hatch, which was finished off with several flat files to remove any bits left by the chisel blade.

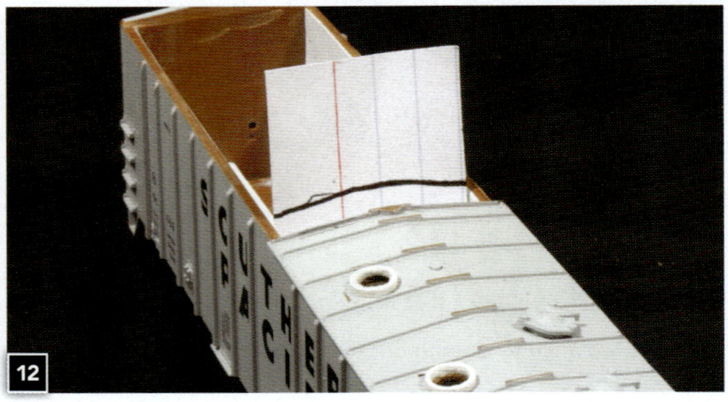

12

Now the basic exterior of the Airslide had been completed, but the real appeal of this scene is the exposed interior. Working from the photo, I determined a simple interior could be constructed from styrene sheet and shapes. I began by placing the floor/underframe components into the molded shell, but leaving them unglued. This enabled me to make a paper template for the wall dividing the interior into two halves as well as the two side walls.

13

Using the templates I cut .015" styrene sheet, then mounted the center wall to the car, tacking it in place with CA. Once dry, I added an .060" x .060" strip reinforcement along the back side before I moved to the side walls. I cemented the sides in place at the top, then I cemented a .060" x .060" strip under the styrene along the bottom edge, creating a slope. A bead of CA created a weld seam.

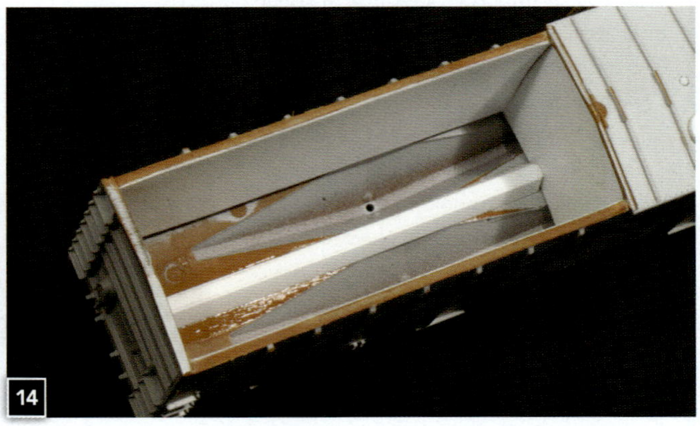

14

After sanding the interior side pieces to blend them in, I turned to the floor. The photo showed it was divided into two sections with a low wall so I glued a strip of Evergreen no. 177 .100" x .156" styrene strip to the center of the floor then added .010" sheet to each side forming a downward slope along each side of the strip. This directed the flow of the contents into the discharge outlets.

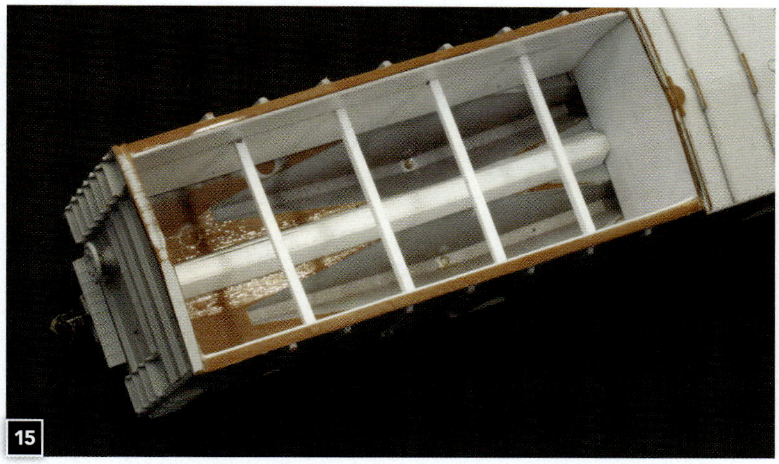

15

Finally it was time to add the last interior component—the interior wall bracing. Although the interior of the Airside is not completely visible in the prototype photo, we can see at least two braces extending between the interior walls. Using the exterior ribs as locations, I cut and glued .060"-square styrene strip between the interior walls, then determined that this looked poor, so I cut another two and cemented them in place as well, making a more visually appealing interior even if slightly inaccurate.

SCRAPPED ROOF

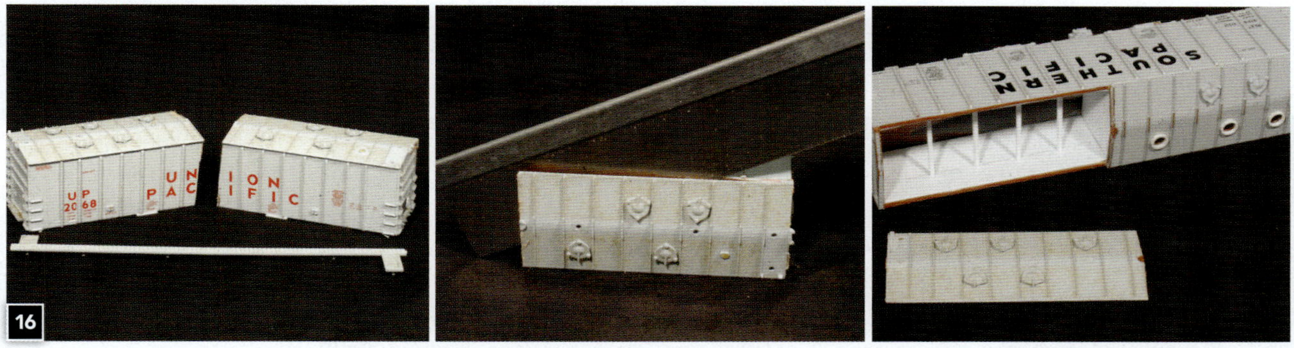

16

Now it was time to turn to the second kit to create the section of roof that had been cut off and laid on the ground beside the car. To remove the roof section I once again located the center of the roof, but this time took a drastically different approach to removing it.

Since I was unconcerned with the carbody I simply cut the entire car in half, then cut alongside the car sides with a razor saw, ensuring I preserved the roof overhang from the car sides, then set aside the remains of the carbody for use later. Next, I filed the roof edges to a bevel to hide the thickness of the molded plastic, then added the hatches intact while leaving the roofwalk off, choosing only to fill the holes for the mounting pins.

17

Having completed all the major bodywork, it was now time for a quick trip into the paint shop where the car interior was airbrushed a flat tan and the exterior was touched up using Testors Light Ghost Gray applied with a brush. I then added a few finishing touches to complete the car, the first was changing the thick solid plastic factory roofwalk to a thin, see-through metal version. I began by filling the mounting holes for the factory roofwalk by cutting the mounting pins from the factory roofwalk and cementing them in place in the holes, providing a solid filler that required very little putty work. I then touched up the paint and added a Plano metal roofwalk that had been a remnant from another project, cementing it to the car using CA applied across the roofwalk mounts.

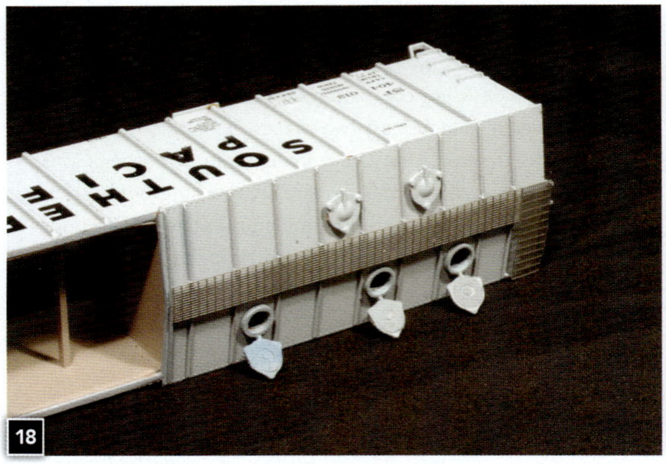

Next I laid the car on its side and added the open hatches, applying CA sparingly to the edges of the collars and hatch hinges.

Finally, I added the remnants of a load to portions of the interior. In studying the prototype photos, there is a small amount of material visible across the interior divider and discharge hoppers. To replicate this, I applied cement, then covered it in Woodland Scenics Fine Buff ballast. Finally, I installed the floor in the car.

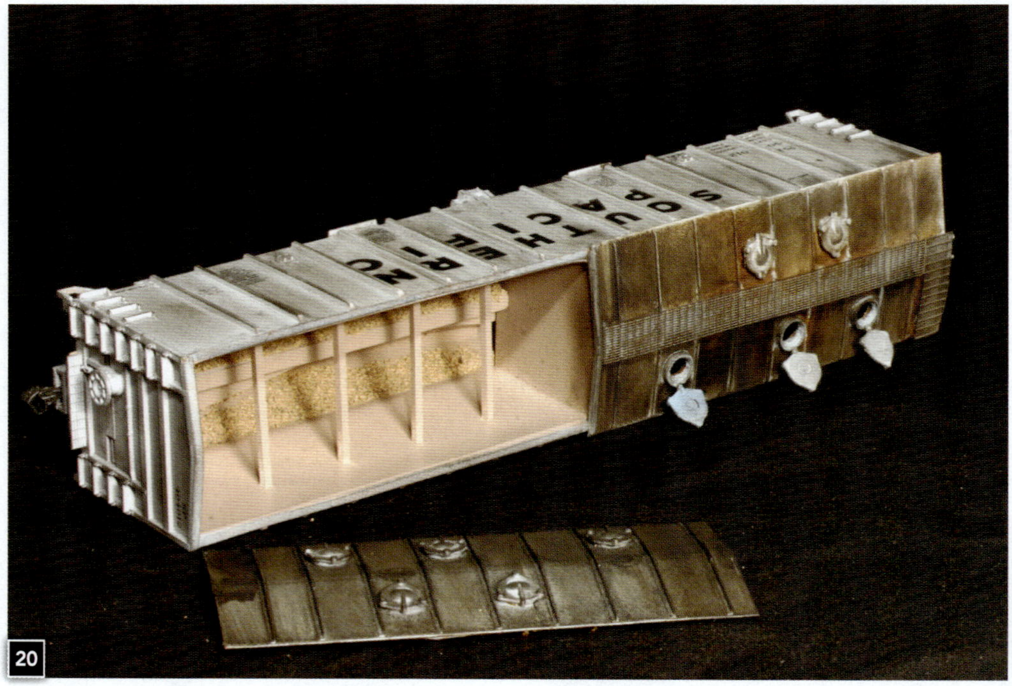

I weathered the car, concentrating on the roof. I began by applying a coating of burnt sienna stamp ink to both sections of roof, followed with an application of black chalk, which gave the roof a rusty texture as well. The exterior sides and ends of the car were given a heavy application of dark brown and black chalks to represent a car that had been in service for almost five decades. weathered the underside heavily with black chalk, partly to hide the lack of detail, then I applied a thin layer of brown chalk to represent rust forming along the top of the interior walls where the lading had never touched.

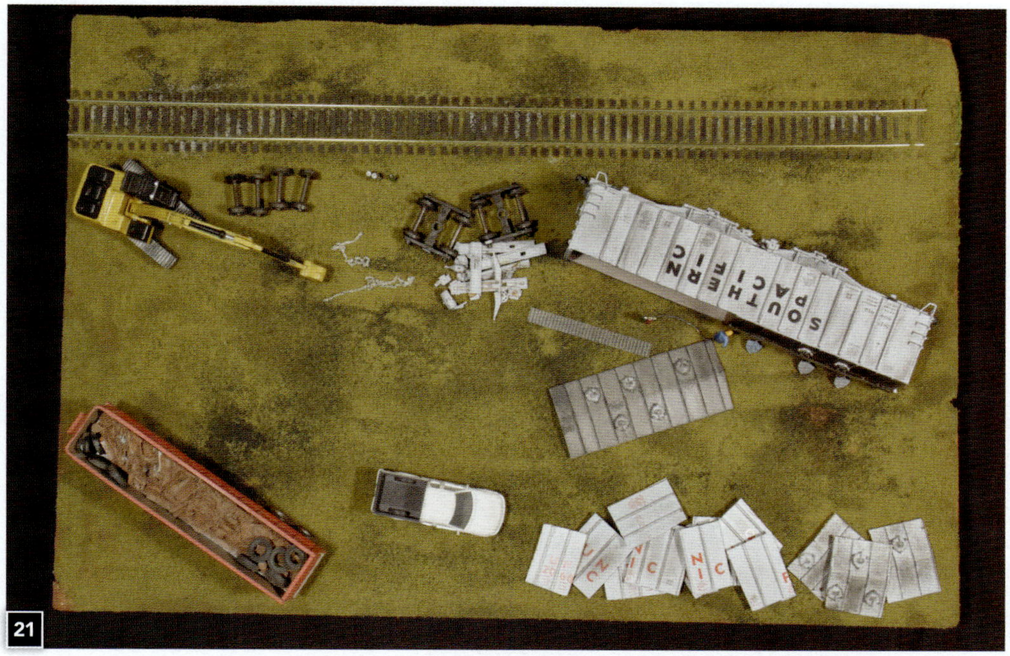

21

Now that we've created a car being dismantled, we look at creating a mobile pop-up scrapping operation you can model on your own layout. As mentioned earlier, this scene requires very little of our precious layout real estate. The scene I created is only 12" x 18" and it could be even further compressed. It requires only nine elements to create it, making it easy and economical as well.

22

Now we will start constructing the scene by adding the first element—the track. In developing this scene, I chose a single track along one side representing a siding that has seen little maintenance, such as an unused team or yard track. I began by painting the rail with a mixture of Rail Brown and Weathered Black, then I brushed a chalk mixture of black and dark gray onto the ties and sealed it. Once this had dried I used a Woodland Scenics Rescue Pad to remove the paint from the top of the rail and restore electrical connectivity, a necessity if locomotives will be operating on the track.

23

With the track ready, I turned to the Styrofoam base on which I constructed the scene and painted the entire area a medium-dark brown. This is always a good idea when doing scenery work as the dark color will camouflage the white base leaving the look of bare soil should any ground foam become lost over time. After this had dried, I coated the area in white glue applied with a sponge brush, spreading it thin and even across the surface of the Styrofoam except for the area of the track. That area was given a thicker coating which would enable me to bury the track,creating the look of a track that rarely sees maintenance.

BURYING TRACK

I then placed the track into the wet glue, allowing the glue to fill the areas between the ties. Next, I applied a puddle of glue over the end of the track, enabling me to create a mound atop the rail that would effectively bury the track. Next a light sprinkling of gray ballast was applied to the track. Then the entire scene was covered in a mixture of Woodland Scenics Earth and Soil ground foam. As the mixture of glue and ground foam dried, I ran a finger along the ties, pushing the foam into the glue and leaving a track that was somewhat buried in the soil of a wide open plot of land.

24

25

Now it was time to add the second element, which is also the anchor model for the scene—the car being dismantled. I placed this at the end of the scene at a slight angle to the track, positioned so the underframe faces away from the viewer and concealing the lack of detail. Adjacent to the car laying on its side I placed the single large piece of roof section that had been removed from the car. I placed it at a different angle, giving the impression it been left laying on the ground to be cut up later.

26

CARRYING A TORCH

Since the theme of the scene is dismantling a railcar, it was time to add the next element, the welder reducing the car into scrap metal. Both Prieser and Woodland Scenics offer excellent figure sets, and I chose the Woodland Scenics set as it included a standing welder, which fit better into the scene I was creating. As a bonus the set included oxygen and acetylene tanks and the appropriate feed hoses, which were installed into holes drilled into the rear of the tanks, and cemented into the arm crook of the figure, creating a single-piece unit of tanks, hose, and figure.

27

I didn't use a torch, but I also cut up the remains of the second Airslide kit that surrendered a section of roof in our first installment. I began by removing the remaining section of roof, then used a razor saw to cut it into several sections parallel with the ribs. Next, I cut each side wall into sections that were no wider than the interior of a gondola. These cuts did not need to be neat and straight. Remember, the worker in the field cut these with a torch. Finally cut all of the smaller parts such as hatches, brake parts, piping components, and trough sections from the sprue, and weather everything to represent components of a car that has been retired after years of service. Then set it all aside.

28

Moving counterclockwise in the scene we can now add some smaller railcar components along with the trucks from the car currently being dismantled. Common amongst most scrap operations, parts that have the potential for resale or rebuilding—such as brake components, wheels and hatch covers—are separated from the parts of the car that are true scrap destined for recycling.

To re-create this, paint the trucks, wheels and axles a dark rust brown, then place them next to the track as if they were rolled back and removed from the track after the car had been laid over. Next to this place the smaller parts cut from the sprue earlier, making a small pile and positioning everything so the exposed sides to the viewer are the "finished" sides.

29

The next element to add is some supply materials. Items such as spare welding canisters and tanks must be kept away from the active work zone for safety reasons, so these are generally staged some distance away. Adding these elements requires no more than adding a few white metal or plastic castings. These can be found through multiple manufacturers including Atlas, Bar Mills, J&L, and Custom Finishing.

Hand in hand with the materials of deconstruction are the materials of removal, namely chains. Large sections of railcar can be easily moved by simply cutting holes in the them and attaching chains, allowing the large bulky pieces to be lifted by various heavy machines such as excavators or heavy duty forklifts. Model chains are available from several manufacturers and a low cost alternative is cheap costume jewelry. Simply find a thin and small linked silver colored necklace chain, cut it into multiple sections of 20 to 30 scale feet, then drybrush them with weathered black or rust to represent steel chains.

30

Moving now to the outer edge of the scene we can complete the first half by adding a heavy duty excavator along with several wheelsets staged in a row, an indicator that this is not the only car that has been scrapped here. While scrap operations often use attachments specially designed to clamp metal components, the basic machines they are mounted on are the same we normally would see in a construction site.

In fact the scrap operation I witnessed used rental excavators with standard digging attachments, utilizing chains wrapped around the bucket to lift the scrap components. With this in mind we can employ any of the myriad of die-cast metal construction models available, such as those offered by Norscot, Atlas, or Herpa, either leaving them stock or kitbashing the specialized attachments.

31

BLUNT AXLES

Next to the heavy-duty equipment we can place several wheelsets, staged and awaiting removal. Unlike our model wheelsets, which feature pointed axles that fit into recesses in the side of the trucks, prototype wheelsets have blunt ends with a bearing that fits into a cutout in the sideframes of the trucks. Modeling this can be done several ways. An economical method is modify older plastic wheel and metal axle sets. Using pliers, grasp the axle behind the wheel and file or grind the point down until it is smooth, resembling the blunt end of a roller bearing. Model trucks that feature rotating roller bearing caps can also be disassembled.

32

Now the first half of the scene is complete and we can continue counterclockwise around the 12" x 18" rectangle adding the seventh element, a dump trailer. While gondolas are perfect for carting away the massive metal sections of railcar, dump trailers can be employed to remove smaller items such as the brake components, which often have a different destination. Ready-to-run dump trailers suitable for scrap steel are available through both Herpa and the Con-Cor Route 66 line which, although largely discontinued, is still plentiful at train shows and auction websites.

Moving to our next element, almost no construction or demolition scene is complete without a pickup. Pickup trucks are available in multiple versions through numerous model manufacturers such as this Ford F150 from Atlas. For a model specifically suited to welding service, a utility body pickup can be outfitted with a welding rig such as the accessory set from River Point Station (part number 537-5253.25).

33

34

Finally we've reached the last element of the scene, pieces from other scrapped cars waiting to be removed. Whether one or more, same body style or not, pieces from another car will give your scene a sense of continuity, showing that this is not the only car that has met its end here.

To complete the utilization of the second kit, I used the remaining wall sections and roof remnants that were cut earlier. On each section simply bevel the rear edges inward to hide the thick plastic, then place them into two groups loosely stacked atop each other, one for wall sections and the second for roof panels.

With our scene complete now we can turn our thoughts to operations. A scene like this can provide near unlimited opportunity as we can utilize nearly any car style—boxcar, hopper, gondola, tank, even locomotives and cabooses—as an inbound load to be disassembled. Likewise we can utilize empty gondolas inbound then turn them into outbound loads filled with railcar scrap requiring nothing more than a quick change between sessions. Best of all it can open up the opportunity to add those roadnames or carbodies you never would have considered before, all while using the bare minimum of space!

CHAPTER EIGHT

Filling in the background

By Dominic Bourgeois // Photos by the author unless otherwise noted

The Delaware & Hudson and Lehigh Valley railroads pooled their six-axle diesels on two pairs of trains beginning in early 1973. Today's run-through MA-2 (Mechanicville, N.Y. – Allentown, Pa.) has drawn a trio of LV C628s from the pool as it attempts to make a run for Richmondville Hill late on a December 1975 afternoon. *Jim Odell, collection of Gardiner Cross*

The same train makes its way across Dominic Bourgeois' HO scale Delaware & Hudson 2nd Subdivision layout. Dominic made extensive use of photos to build his model railroad.

WHAT'S IN THE PHOTO

1. Signals on cantilever mast
2. Borst & Burhans flour mill
3. France Milling Co.
4. Line poles
5. Signal cabinet

The object of my modeling has long been the representation of the northern portion of the Delaware & Hudson's 2nd Subdivision main line, circa 1975, in the most exact and realistic manner possible in HO scale. I have previously built models of other locations along the line, notably downtown Schenectady, N.Y., but the last few years have been devoted to replicating a slice of Cobleskill, N.Y.

After completing the area best known and most often photographed by railfans, which includes the ornate station and the iconic Cobleskill Coal Company, I shifted my attention to the area to the southwest of the coal dealer. This swath of the town includes several mills and a creamery.

While railfans seldom walk in that direction, some of the structures dominate the background of photos taken at the coal company. I resolved to pursue my philosophy of deviating as little as possible from reality and included the mills on my model, despite their non-traffic-generating status in my chosen era.

Interestingly, while I model a relatively recent era, the structures in

Mock-ups

The mill model was huge and visually overwhelming. "In your face" would be an apt description. The reality is that I had painted myself into a corner and was not inclined to significantly deviate from the prototype. I therefore built the mill anyway, assuming that some of the bulk inherent in the all-white mock-up would be lessened by the actual model's dark-colored slate roof and red brick boiler room annex.

And I was correct: Now that it's finished, painted and weathered, the mill seems to adequately recede into the scene. The turnouts are still behind it, but they can be seen from the ends without excessive stretching, and they form part of an industry lead, not the main line, so the associated risks are less.

They are controlled by toggles at the front edge of the layout and feature rotating switch stand targets, thereby giving operators a chance to assess their positions from indirect vantage points. The signal is also back there, but it thankfully extends above the boiler room annex's roofline and is sufficiently visible. Engineers will have to pay close attention in order not to bypass it, however.

this scene are all vestiges of earlier times and therefore feature the kind of neglect and decay one often sees on Depression-era layouts. I normally avoid over-weathering my structures, but in this case it is appropriate. Note, however, that most of the apparent aging is only as deep as the paint (or lack thereof); the buildings were still somewhat maintained at the time. In fact, most of them survive largely intact even today.

Proto-freelancers often play up the perceived value of their approach by stating that it is much harder to create a credible freelanced model scene than it is to dumbly copy a prototype one. While they are correct about the challenging nature of their approach, there are also significant difficulties and potential pitfalls inherent in stricter prototype modeling which also requires extensive thought and planning.

For example, when taking inspiration from the prototype, you would think that scene composition would be taken care of by default. That would be an incorrect assumption. Since we usually must compress prototype scenes to successfully nest them in our universally inadequate spaces, their elements often must be compressed, slid around relative to each other, or otherwise contorted in some way.

Some items might even need to be eliminated altogether to make the most desirable ones fit, but great care is required to ensure they are not missed, especially in highly recognizable prototype scenes. Even in obscure locations, there is a risk that the remaining elements might not juxtapose well if something between them is amiss or the intervening space is inadequate.

Another result of limited space is the necessity to twist our trackage to fit the confines of the layout room, preferably in a way that does not betray the rather linear nature of the prototype. My scene is, in reality, stretched along a long, broad convex curve when seen from the aisle.

I was able to correctly represent the beginning of that curve near the well-known coal company, but here between the mills I had to revert to a tangent alignment before turning the main in the opposite direction to avoid having the main line bump into the backdrop.

Another prosaic challenge has to do with access: Some features of a prototype scene may be hard to reach for construction, maintenance, or operation when scaled down to a model context. Creativity must almost always be exercised to resolve such issues.

In my case, two mills and a creamery conveniently belonged along the background of the scene. All were truncated against the backdrop to some extent, though I always seek to preserve the roof ridge by increasing the steepness of the roof slope if I have to, essentially foreshortening the walls that are perpendicular to the aisle.

The prototype dictated that the former Borst & Burhans buckwheat flour mill be located along the front of the layout, between the aisle and the trackage. For smaller structures, that is usually not much of an issue, but this particular model, despite having been compressed somewhat, measures nearly 2 actual feet long and is quite tall, thereby having a significant impact on visibility and access.

A spur and a couple of turnouts are located behind it and, even worse, so is a mainline signal gantry. On the prototype, some of these features actually aren't behind the building, but my limited space forced them much closer together. I didn't worry so much about that drawback when I first drew the track plan and then handlaid the track (read between the lines: It didn't occur to me that there was a problem), but the issue came to the forefront, literally, when I mocked up the mill to check its impact. I was disappointed.

Site and terrain

The modeled terrain is not quite flat. There is a slight slope up from the front edge to the backdrop, and I felt it was important to represent that feature. It is not obvious to the casual observer, but the level change can be perceived in low-angle photos.

Because the track and multiple buildings must all sit on flat surfaces, the benchwork surface is built as a series of tiers. The mainline sits on ¼"-thick cork roadbed, itself glued to ½" plywood. The foreground industry lead sits on the same level of plywood as the main, but it uses thinner roll cork to drop it down slightly relative to the mainline. It also consists of code 70 rail, as opposed to the main's code 83, to further differentiate them.

The foreground mill and a couple of spurs sit directly on ¼" plywood, therefore a bit lower than the lead. The spurs have no ballast. They are completely engulfed in tall grass to convey their disuse. On the far side of the main line, there is a slice of space from a long-removed spur. It gradually ascends along its length.

Because the ½" plywood extends to the backdrop, ¼" foam core was used for its roadbed, while cereal-box cardboard built up in layers underneath establishes the slope. The surface is covered by a mixture of cinders, grass, weeds and shrubs, portraying an abandonment that is in a distant past.

Finally, the rear buildings also sit on built-up layers of foam core, each at a slightly different elevation along the sloped spur. The signal gantry visible at right is a stand-in I move from scene to scene as I build. I only replace it with the finished model as the end of construction nears.

Structures

1

2

1. There's no getting around the fact that prototype modeling requires most structures to be scratchbuilt or at least extensively kitbashed from commercial offerings. While I do sometimes balk at the sheer amount of work that entails, after the fact I feel great satisfaction in the result, which is unlike what can be found on any other layout. Seeing a Heljan brewery or Walthers Northern Power & Light kit for the umpteenth time on a layout does little to conjure a feeling of realism, not for lack of quality or skill, but simply because of their ubiquity.

With the exception of some famous locations, kits for the necessary buildings are typically non-existent. I measured and then scratchbuilt the coal company's bunker, but as luck would have it plans for it were later published in the model press and a kit released soon thereafter, but that is a truly rare occurrence.

While I do measure key structures, most models are based off guesstimated dimensions. In fact, some degree of compression is usually applied. I often prepare drawings of my buildings, but they are generally very basic elevations whose function is mainly to establish critical roof geometry.

2. I try to work on my models in subassemblies, keeping the walls separate until they are fully painted and detailed, often even weathered, before finally assembling them. Yes, I test fit them together with painters' tape as work progresses, but I find that painting and detailing are much easier to do on flat surfaces than on cumbersome 3D assemblies.

Liquid solvent cement readily cuts through the (now-discontinued) Polly Scale paint I use, but if not, I use a hobby knife to scratch away the paint on the surfaces to be joined. Paint touch-ups are sometimes necessary after assembly, but not always if one is careful.

The Borst & Burhans mill's walls feature some interesting aged paint effects. They were reproduced by either painting the walls white and drybrushing gray streaks, or the exact opposite, depending on the area. White and gray color pencils, further drybrushing, washes, and powders were all used to add more distress and tie everything together. The lettering was printed on clear decal sheet, applied to the surface, and weathered along with the rest of the wall. Challenges like this are among the reasons I truly enjoy prototype modeling. They add tremendous interest to prototype models.

3. Doors and windows are usually drawn directly on the brick sheet or wood siding. In the latter case, where I use Evergreen Scale Models sheets, I will cut them out either to fit commercial castings or, more commonly, make the openings to a size that includes the sill, jambs and head of my scratchbuilt windows.

HO scale 4x4 strip styrene is used for the jambs and head, while 1x6 or 2x6 strips are used for the sill and drip above the head.

Styrene .020" thick is then placed behind the window opening, which is traced onto it with a sharp pencil, and the glazed opening is cut about a scale 2" inside the lines to leave perimeter sashes.

3

4

A scale 2x2 is then glued across the opening at mid-height. After painting, clear styrene is glued behind the window opening (also easier done before the walls are assembled together). The windows are usually subdivided by scribing mullions in the clear styrene, and appropriately colored pastel chalk is rubbed into the scribed lines to color them.

For Borst & Burhans, I mostly used Tichy castings because I didn't feel like scratchbuilding the more than 60 windows required, but most other structures, notably France Milling, have scratchbuilt windows.

Doors are framed in the same manner as windows, but in their case .005" styrene is laminated to a .020" sheet, the former cut out as necessary to represent paneling.

4. In brick walls, the JTT Scenery Products TT scale brick sheet (closer to correct size than the HO version) is cut out to accommodate the windows, but also the stone or concrete sills (scale 4 x 4 or 4 x 6 styrene) and, if present, the brick arches.

The brick is laminated to .030" styrene after the window openings are cut out, again leaving 2" sashes all around. The arches are made by cutting 2/3 of the way through a strip of brick, between each brick. That action naturally curves the arch and it is then cut to the proper length and glued on.

The entire wall is painted a natural brick color (boxcar red and/or rust – NOT red). Mortar joints are simulated with a wash of beige pastel chalk (NOT white) and the surface is rubbed with a moist paper towel to remove the excess. (A white-on-red combination yields pink brick, which looks terrible to me.) Weathering is done with chalks, but colored pencils are also used to vary the color of individual bricks.

The roof consists of Plastruct asphalt shingle patterned sheet laminated to .040" styrene. On select structures, I prefer to apply individual shingle strips, but the roof surface area of this building was significant, so I opted for the less labor-intensive approach. The patterned sheets are somewhat coarse, so judicious applications of paint, washes, pencil shingle highlights, and chalk weathering are critical to achieving a realistic finish.

5

When the building was finally assembled, its foundation was traced onto 1⁄16" mat board, which was then cut out and glued to the layout surface. This provides a flat surface for the model to sit on and simplified the application of scenery around the building.

6

As had been hoped for, the final painted building looks far less bulky than its mock-up.

Track, ballast, and ground cover

My track is handlaid. Some modern commercial track products are more realistic than the hand-built variety, but I still make my own for convenience and to obtain tighter tolerances at switch points. Pros and cons are that my track has less detail and it's more work, but it costs less and is more adaptable to odd situations.

For instance, I have built many no. 7 turnouts, which are not available commercially. One turnout near the creamery and visible in the photo is "abandoned;" it leads to a long-removed track and its points are spiked in place.

The mainline curves are superelevated by gluing a narrow strip of 1⁄16" mat board under the outer end of the ties. The transition from flat to superelevated is accomplished by layering strips of masking tape of progressively shorter length until the full height is attained, with the overall 18" length approximately corresponding to the length of the spiral transition between tangent and the constant-radius curve while being long enough to avoid hampering the tracking characteristics of the rolling stock, which is obviously critical.

The built-up tape is wide, but it is sliced into narrow strips, yielding enough material for several transitions. The main line is ballasted with now-discontinued Highball ballast, a mix of its HO scale light and dark grays. The industry lead track is embedded in its N scale cinders (all yard tracks in Cobleskill are so treated).

I applied a streak of black pastel chalk to the centerline of each mainline track to simulate oil and grime. The spur tracks in this scene see very little use, so they are overgrown with weeds.

Some of the low grasses and weeds are electrostatic grass fibers from Silflor, but the bulk of that vegetation consists of short static grass flock from Woodland Scenics, as well as its Field Grass fibers, cut to random length with scissors and applied onto diluted white glue by hand one small clump at a time. It's time-consuming, but the technique better represents dead or tamped-down fall grasses than the use of electrostatic devices.

Orange-brown ground foam was applied randomly and sparingly to represent fallen leaves, especially under trees and in locations where wind would drop them.

Trees

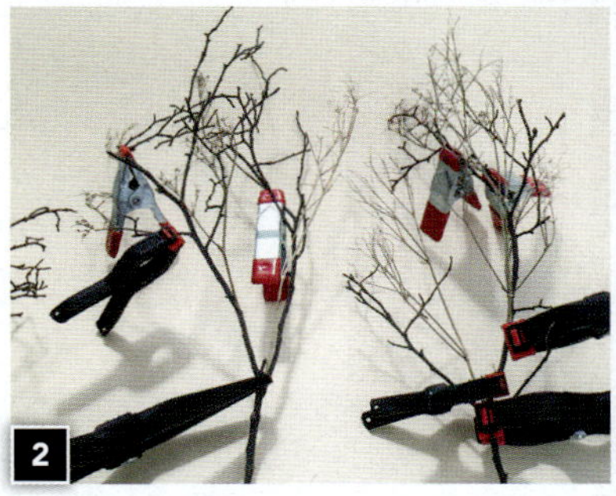

1. I use natural branches, picked during the winter and carefully selected to appear like scale tree trunks and main limbs. Modeling late autumn entails that the trees are often bare, so it is necessary to add finer branch structures to the basic armatures. Dollar stores and art supply dealers sometimes sell packaged dried sage, often stained, which has a reasonably fine structure but still has countless buds attached. They can work if ground foam "leaves" are added. And of course Scenic Express Super Trees can also work well, though I have yet to try them myself.

2. For bare or almost bare trees, though, I use baby's breath. I let it dry over a few months and then pull off the tiny flowers. I laboriously glue each branch to the main armature using white glue and small clamps to hold them in place while the glue dries. For some reason, cyanoacrylate adhesive (CA) doesn't seem to work very well for this, but hot glue would be an option. The stems are cut at an angle, the cut surface becoming the joint face against the armature. After the joints dry, more glue is built up to reinforce them and to hide the cut ends. Gray and dark brown spray paint unifies and trues the color.

3. One of the benefits of the late-fall setting is that I can exercise foliage control: I can reduce or eliminate leaves where it is important for features to be visible. I did this with the low trees in front of France Milling, which are much denser on the prototype, so the doors and windows I'd spent so much effort building remain visible. The foreground tree was left bare to minimize its visual impact.

Relay cases

I took pains to document the General Railway Signal relay cases, signal equipment, and other trackside details along the D&H right-of-way many years ago. Many of these details have since been replaced by subsequent owners Canadian Pacific and now Norfolk Southern, so I'm really glad I did. I use a handy 12"-square piece of cardstock with 6", 3", and 1" markings. Along with a good flat-on photo, that is all I need to make close-enough-to-scale drawings of relatively small items.

I built a stockpile of GRS relay cases before 3D printing became viable, but I would probably use the new technology for this application were I doing it today.

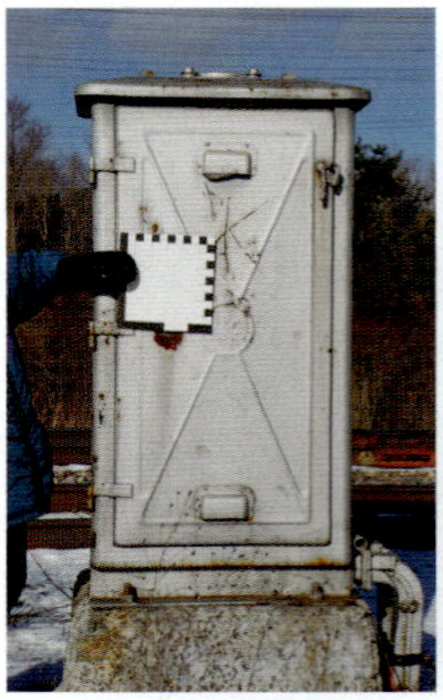

Signals

Like the relay cases, I started stockpiling scratchbuilt signal components years ago and would also likely use 3D printing today, at least for the plastic gantries. The individual signal masts consist of brass tubing, to which three-lead, two-color 3mm LEDs are soldered (at the center, i.e. ground, lead). I use two home-built wood jigs to solder the brass assemblies together, including platforms, railings, and Walthers signal ladder stock. One jig is used with the signals face-down, while the other accommodates the signals on their side. Each is used for specific steps in the assembly.

The finished signals and other appliances are painted silver, as the Delaware & Hudson started doing around 1973-74. I apply a clear flat finish over the silver paint to tone it down a little. Note that this particular signal gantry features a non-standard extension of the beam in order to support a dummy/placeholder mast, since there is an unsignalled track (the industry lead) between the gantry's base and the main tracks, which are governed by the signal heads.

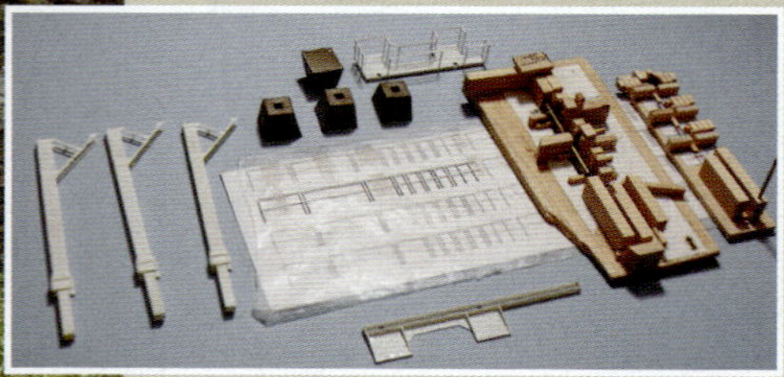

My signals are functional, driven by home-built logic circuits. I am going to use Arduinos in the future, since they are inexpensive and very flexible, and, importantly, compatible with my existing circuits. I learned the Pascal programming language in college decades ago, and the Arduino C++ coding is similar enough to minimize my learning curve.

Switch stands

Rotating switch stand targets help operators determine switch positions in less visible locations. A wire rod is soldered to the underside of the PC board throwbar and its free end is bent up and offset from center to mate with the switch stand, **1**.

Micro Engineering switch stands are modified by adding a thin styrene base plate under the stock base, with a smaller diameter hole than the existing one for the vertical rod to pass through. The lever arm is a small length of styrene strip with rounded ends and two holes in it, **2**.

The distance between the holes translates the linear motion of the points into a 90 degree rotation. My points-to-stock rail gap is about 6 scale inches. A bit of high school-level trigonometry (6"/2/sin 45°) establishes a scale 4.24" spacing of the holes.

Cutting a rounded notch in one of the switch ties is often required to provide adequate clearance for the lever arm's motion. Make no mistake: This is finicky work requiring a lot of adjustment to pull off successfully, but it's a joy when it finally works as intended, **3** and **4**.

1

2

3

4

1

Details

1. My modeled scene features very little detail beyond what's part of the structures and the right-of-way hardware. There was a surprising boost in realism when I added the lineside poles, however, which are from Rix Products. I remove some insulators to match the real thing, then painted them, making sure to weather the crossarms more than the poles, paint the diagonal straps a galvanized metal color, and the insulators a blue-green color, with some in light gray, again to approximate the prototype.

I do not string wires in the poles for three reasons: They are on the near side of the tracks and thus susceptible to being snagged; I find the lack of proper wire sagging less realistic than the outright absence of wires; and my model of Cobleskill consists of portable modules that I move from time to time. Were the poles located on the far side of the tracks, there would be one less reason not to string wires, so I might consider it on a permanent layout.

2

2. There's one little pile of debris near the creamery, but otherwise no "junk" is to be found anywhere. I personally find strewing junk everywhere to be unrealistic. Sure, you will find clusters of organized or haphazard outdoor storage in places, but it is nowhere near as commonplace as modelers tend to feature. I just include what I see in period photos, which is not all that much. In this case, less is more.

That being said, I plan on adding a few more details here and there, such as some portable propane cylinders and perhaps some burlap bags at the Borst & Burhans streetside dock, and maybe some old, discarded ties along the track somewhere, but little else. (A pickup is normally parked in front of the mill, but my model is of a slightly more recent vintage than my modeled era, so I removed it for the photos.)

While I still need to model the outskirts of town, with the completion of this scene my miniature version of downtown Cobleskill is fully realized.

CHAPTER NINE

Building an offline customer

By James McNab // Photos by the author unless otherwise noted

Hills Grain and Feed strikes a towering figure in the skyline of Hills, Iowa. The variety of bins and buildings present makes the prototype structure an excellent option for a variety of layout concepts and designs.

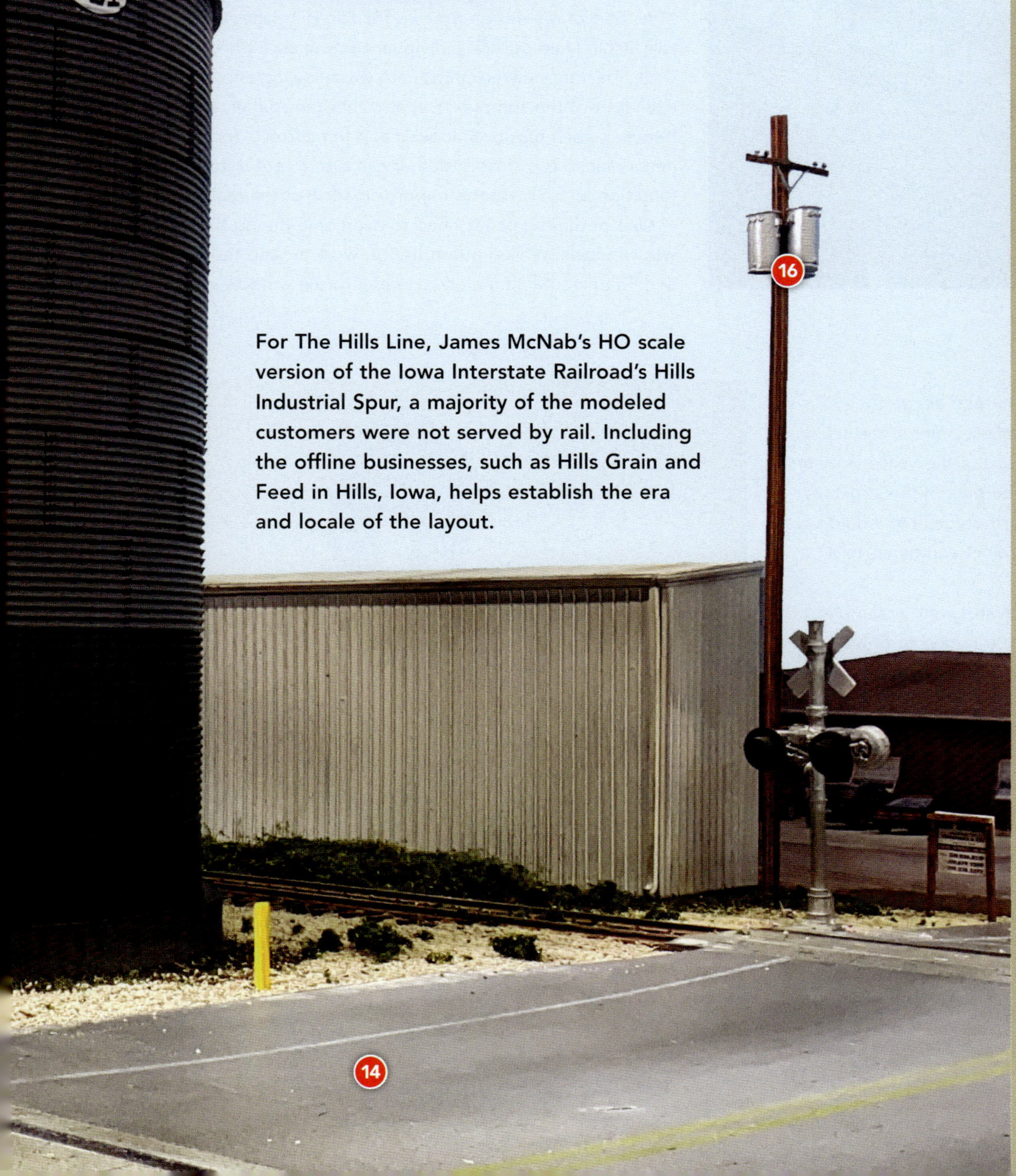

For The Hills Line, James McNab's HO scale version of the Iowa Interstate Railroad's Hills Industrial Spur, a majority of the modeled customers were not served by rail. Including the offline businesses, such as Hills Grain and Feed in Hills, Iowa, helps establish the era and locale of the layout.

WHAT'S IN THE PHOTO

1. Wet/dry bin
2. Four small grain bins
3. Elevator
4. Two large grain bins
5. Main Street
6. Rooftop auger
7. Power pole with transformer
8. Crossing flashers
9. Storage warehouse
10. Wet/dry bin—Rix Products bin with styrene support structure
11. Four small grain bins—Rix Products grain bins
12. Elevator— Walthers Valley Growers Association
13. Two large grain bins—Walthers Big Grain Storage Bins
14. Main Street—.040" PLA styrene
15. Rooftop auger—Bossen Implement auger kit
16. Power pole with transformer— bamboo kabob skewers with Rix Products crossarms and Bar Mills transformers

There are 16 identified businesses or industries on The Hills Line, my HO scale version of the Iowa Interstate's Hills Industrial Spur in eastern Iowa. Of that number, only two were served by rail during my modeled era. That means a majority of the buildings are there for looks alone, and do not contribute toward the operating scheme of the layout.

At first glance, that may seem like a significant imbalance, especially considering the desire of most modelers and operators to squeeze as much potential from our layouts as possible. But the prototype Hills Line was the definition of less being more. On average a train would serve the line only twice per week to switch either or both of the online customers. During that trip the crew would move less than a dozen cars in total.

So my modeled version needed to include a lot of structures that helped set the era and locale, and did nothing more. By far the largest and most visible offline industry is Hills Grain and Feed, the municipal grain elevator complex in the industrial spur's namesake town. Since the business has such a significant physical presence in Hills, and is both surrounded as well as bisected by the railroad, it deserved to be replicated in the best manner possible.

Planning the spot

Hills Grain and Feed is positioned alongside the industrial spur at the north side of the small hamlet of Hills, Iowa. A siding splits the complex, separating the elevator from the grain bins. The main thoroughfare through town, the aptly named Main Street, crosses perpendicular to both the running track and the siding, forming the southern border of the scene.

As part of my design process for The Hills Line, and the town of Hills itself, I laid out the individual components while I was laying track. This not only ensured that I was allowing enough space for each part of the complex, but also that the spatial relationships between each part both looked and felt correct. Too many items placed too close together can turn a prototypically correct rendition into a cartoonish approximation of the real world.

One of the big issues I had to overcome during the design phase was windows. While I attempted to work around them, Hills Grain and Feed would ultimately extend into the window space.

A central point

Since the elevator building would extend above the backdrop, as well as serve as the tallest point in the scene, it felt like a natural starting point. I used the Valley Growers Association kit from Walthers for the bulk of the structure, since it was a close match to the prototype, and would save time on constructing the overall project compared to a completely scratchbuilt version.

The three visible sides of the elevator were assembled following the instructions, but were trimmed to fit into my available space. I've found that a strong utility knife with a fresh blade makes quick work of cutting into commercial plastics and styrene. The walls were glued and secured with Tamiya extra thin modeler's cement.

For the unseen back wall I used artists foamboard to fill the gap. The partially completed elevator was traced onto the board to form an inset. This blank was then placed inside the elevator and secured with hot glue, both to provide support to the building, but also to prevent any light leaks from happening due to its close proximity to the basement window.

Because I use J-channel trim on the edges of my backdrop in lieu of a valance, the elevator would be prevented from sitting flush with the back of the scene. I notched the two side walls with a styrene nibbler to clear the trim pieces.

I temporarily left off the roof pieces of the building, as well as the window glass inserts, to avoid having to mask the pieces during painting. Fortunately I discovered that the large sign atop the elevator, present in the prototype photo, was not added until well after my modeled era. That meant I could skip having to make it from dry-transfer letters or custom decals.

Supporting structures

The remaining buildings alongside the elevator are not much more than simple boxes. The two low storage warehouses were kitbashed from a Pikestuff Pre-Fab Warehouse kit, since it was a near perfect match to the prototype. I made a pair of backdrop flats by cutting the pieces in half with an utility knife. Any joints were covered with the modeled downspouts included with the kit.

For the dryer building, I started with a section of PVC trim board to serve as the core. JTT Scenery Products concrete-block sheets were then attached with construction adhesive and some drops of cyanoacrylate adhesive (CA). I added corner trim pieces from Plastruct styrene shapes, along with some cap tiles from Pikestuff attached to the edges of the roof.

To help simulate the tar paper and gravel roof, I used a sheet of 120 grit sandpaper cut to size. I've come to prefer this material for modeling flat roofs, since it gives me more control and a better appearance than trying to use real rock or ballast. The sandpaper was painted with a dark gray spray paint primer, and glued to the top of the core with CA.

Gathering the grain

Hills Grain and Feed features a motley collection of grain bins in various heights and diameters. To replicate the variety present, I turned to a similarly-assorted selection of commercial products.

The two large bins on the south end of the complex were made from Walthers Big Grain Storage Bins, **1** and **2**. Since the prototype features a different vent style than the one provided in the kit, I needed to fill the included holes in the roof since I wouldn't be using them. I attached the included vent pieces to the top of the bin, then cut them flush with the roof to plug the holes. Tamiya Putty was used to fill the seams, then sanded smooth when dry.

Rix Products oft-used grain bins made up the bulk of the complex, **3**. The four shorter units were built following the included directions, including adding the appropriate detail parts. The kits allowed me to customize the height to fit my needs, but were otherwise built as designed. I made sure to line up the seams, alternating between bands as I assembled each layer. Be sure to take your time and line up the individual corrugations as well while gluing them together.

For the lone bin at the north end of the industry, I wanted to try something different, since it would stand out more than the rest of the bins. My friends at Iowa Scaled Engineering released a version of the prototype in HO scale under their Grain Belt Models line, **4**. Their products have the advantage of being built as complete rings instead of separate pieces, which makes assembly considerably quicker. Grain Belt Models markets this 18-foot version as the Hills bin.

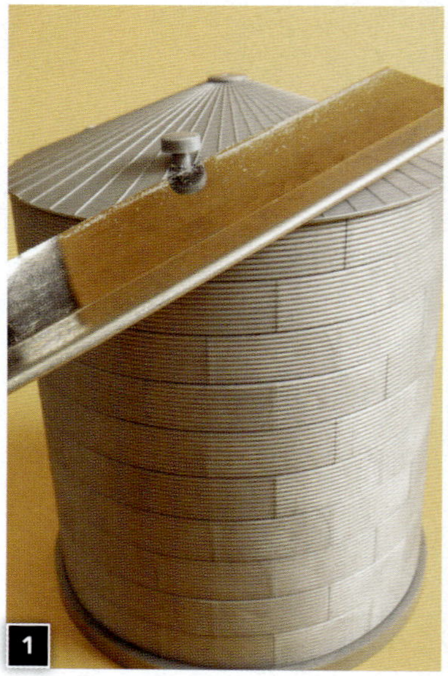

1

2

3

4

The custom wet-dry bin

1

2

3

The remaining bin, a large wet-dry storage version, offered a unique challenge. The prototype is smaller than a lot of commercially-available options, so much so that kitbashing the bin from those products would ultimately not offer as accurate of a representation. I assembled my own version using a variety of scratchbuilding supplies.

Since the wet-dry bin matched the other, smaller bins in the complex, I used another Rix Products version as the start for my custom arrangement. One of their 15 degree tank tops was applied to the bottom of the completed structure to seal up the bin, **1**.

I then applied Plastruct styrene C-channel pieces to the sides to model the legs, **2**. Six separate strips were attached evenly around the entire bin, and extended 2 inches below the bottom of the bin.

Separate .040" strips from Evergreen Scale Models between the legs serve as cross braces to stabilize the entire structure, **3**. However, I did not add footings, since they would be covered by grass, weeds, and other underbrush once installed on the layout.

Details galore

A plethora of smaller detail parts were then added to the entire complex. While none of the grain bins are connected to each other, as often happens in larger setups, each bin does include the typical set of accessories such as chutes, dryers, and access doors.

Rix Products' Grain Bin Parts accessory kits were used on all the bins in the complex, based on prototype placement.

Following prototype practice, roof access supports were added using Evergreen styrene strips. They were attached to the bin top with Tamiya Extra Thin cement.

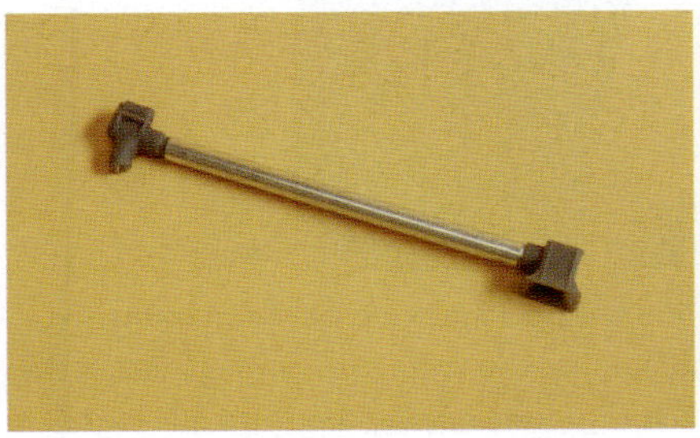

One of the key details is the large roof auger that sits atop the grain bin at the southern end of the scene. Despite searching for a suitable product, I was never able to locate an appropriate version in HO scale. I finally lucked out when I discovered an auger kit from Bossen Implement, a farm toy dealer located in eastern Iowa. While the kit is scaled at 1/64th of full size (S scale), I was able to cut down the main tube to better fit my 1/87th scale needs. The supports for the auger atop the bin were shaped from .025" piano wire.

The remaining items came from my ever-growing collection of scrap and detail parts. I referenced prototype photos for the style and placement of all the parts, knowing I can always come back later and add or remove as information becomes available.

Paint, weathering, and decals

With construction complete, each of the parts of the overall complex were then individually painted and weathered. I prefer to use spray paint for the majority of my model paint needs, since it offers a far-greater quantity at a far-lower price. The variety of colors available from your local hardware shop rivals the best-stocked hobby store.

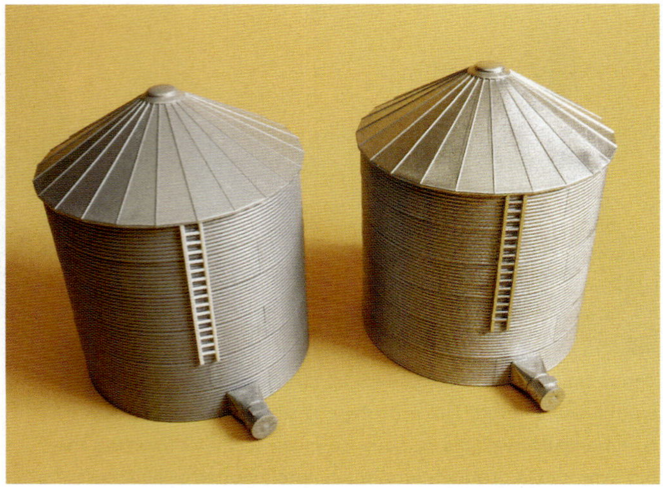

Each part was painted in a base primer color to prep for weathering. Spray paints are available in a variety of hues and tints to match whatever look you're trying to achieve.

For weathering I generally use two materials: PanPastel powders and an India ink and isopropyl alcohol wash. PanPastels can quickly be applied using makeup or foam brushes, and do an excellent job of working their way into the smallest nooks and crevices. The India ink wash, applied with an airbrush, can quickly tone down even the most vibrant colors.

I started the weathering process with PanPastels on the roofs, since they generally have the highest concentration of rust, dirt, and grime. I then worked down the sides of the buildings to highlight individual details.

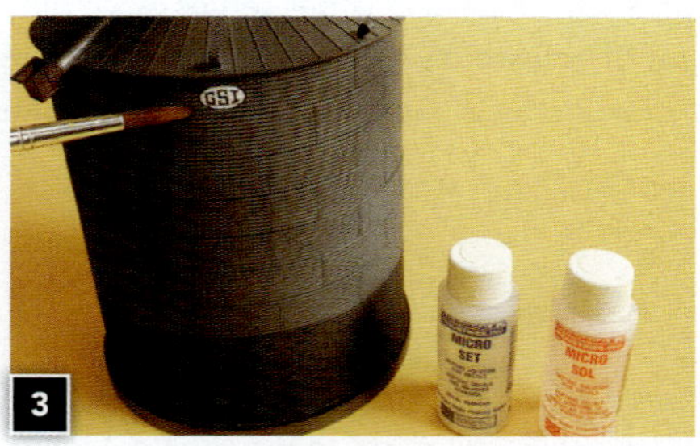

For more precise applications, I used eyeshadow brushes to work the powders into small areas, **1**. PanPastels help bring out the detail of the support bracing on the wet-dry bin. After applying a layer of Dullcote to set the powders and letting it fully dry, I finished up with the India ink wash to blend everything together. The combination of the two offers a realistic look to my modeled structures.

For the distinctive darker band on the large grain bins, I masked a portion of the structure with tape, leaving the lower sections uncovered, **2**. I then reapplied the India Ink wash to the bottom of the bins. The tape gave me a crisp separation between layers.

While I previously mentioned that the large sign on the sides of the elevator was not present in my modeled era, there are still logos on several of the bins and buildings, **3**. Fortunately, Grain Belt Models offers a variety of custom decals appropriate for modern-era agriculture structures. I used both Micro Set and Micro Sol setting solutions to work the decals in-between the corrugations of the bins. Additional caution and warning signs were applied where appropriate throughout the complex.

The main drag

1

Over the years, I've tried a variety of products for modeling roads on a model railroad, from plaster to foamboard to even paper. I've come to prefer both the consistency and flexibility that styrene sheet provides. I can create everything from a single-lane backwoods road to a multi-lane freeway from the same material and using the same methods. Streets, curbs, and sidewalks can all be made at one time from the same material.

The key to making effective styrene roads is to use as large of a piece as possible so that seams and joints are either minimized or eliminated. Fortunately commercial plastic suppliers offer 4x8 foot sheets at a considerable cost savings over hobby-sized pieces. I picked up a sheet of .040" PLA styrene from a local provider for less than $30. After sketching out the rough plan, I cut the styrene using a the Plasticutter scribe tool from MicroMark, a utility knife, and a pair of stout scissors.

2

The completed roadway was then spray-painted with the cheapest flat gray primer I could find to serve as the base asphalt color. Similar but separate shades of gray were used to replicate both asphalt and concrete sections.

3

I followed by masking off the road stripes with blue painter's tape, then applied yellow and white acrylic craft paints with a foam brush to paint in the markings. A light dabbing motion with the foam brush helped create a more weathered look to the stripes.

4

As a final step, I blended everything together with the same India Ink wash I used on the structures. Individual exhaust streaks were modeled by running the airbrush down the center of the lane. Once dry, I attached the finished road to the layout using foam-safe construction adhesive.

Crossing protection

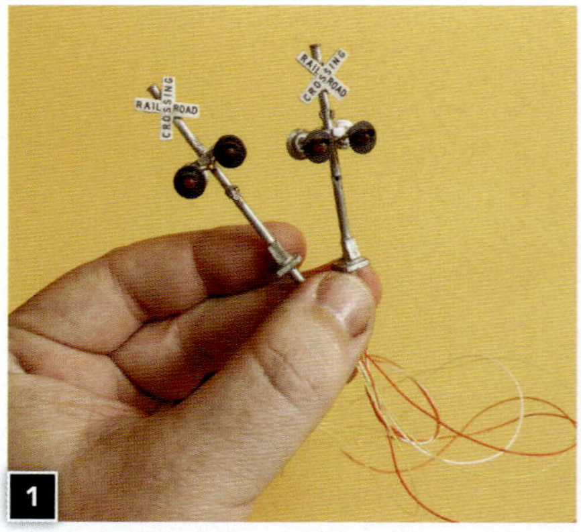

1

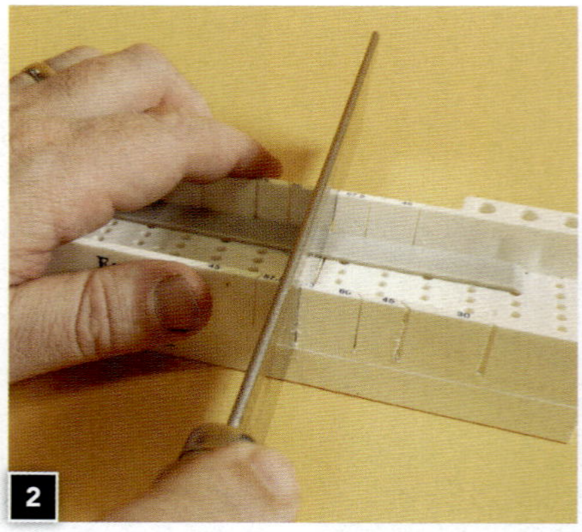
2

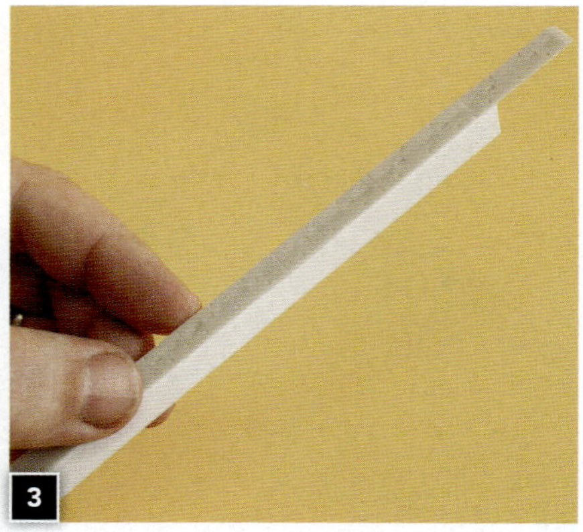
3

Since Main Street in Hills crosses over both the industrial spur and the siding, I needed to provide protection for both motorists and railroad crews. On the prototype, a set of crossbucks with flashers protect each track, **1**. Tomar Industries signals were used on both crossings, while the Grade Crossing Pro circuit from Logic Rail Technologies was used for realistic operation of the flashers. Functioning signals also provide a level of kinetic energy to the scene.

The crossing's panels were from the Walthers Modern Concrete Grade Crossing kit, **2**. For the base color I painted them with Testor's Flat Light Aircraft Gray, since it does a good job of simulating fresh concrete on its own. The India ink wash was again used to tone down the paint and blend the crossing in with the roads.

Scrap pieces of styrene were used to shim both the crossing pieces and the roads so that they were flush and level with each other, **3**. That way Main Street flows smoothly across the track, just as on the prototype.

For miles and miles

1

2

Despite the scene being only 16 inches deep, it's possible to extend it beyond the layout's boundaries through the use of photo backdrops, **1**. Thanks to modern geo-mapping software, such as Google Streetview and Bing Streetside, I was able to capture a view of Main Street in Hills without having to travel to the location to photograph it in person.

The individual images were manipulated in Adobe Photoshop, mostly to remove the sky as well as clean up the sometimes rough edges of structures caused by the photo-capture process. An overall panorama was generated and printed out onto individual sheets, **2**. Once the excess was trimmed, I mounted the pictures to the backdrop using photo-safe glue.

3

I generally prefer to match the photo to the model, not the other way around. I find it considerably simpler to modify colors on an image in Photoshop than to modify colors on a physical road with paint. However, I did use PanPastel powders to help blend the line between the three-dimensional foreground and the two-dimensional background, further blurring the transition point, **3**.

It's electric

1

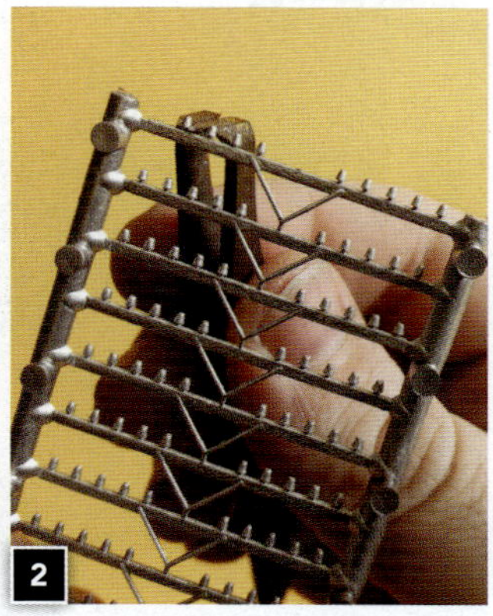

2

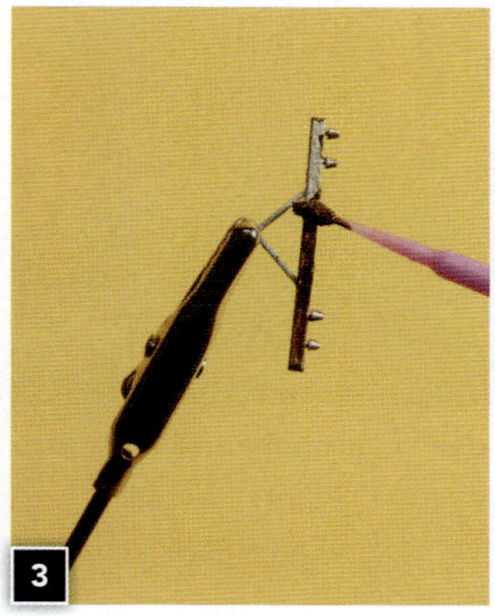

3

4

One of the simplest detail parts to make are also one of the most ubiquitous ones found in the real world. Utility poles have been present for as long as railroads have, so including them in our model scenes is both accurate and appropriate.

The photo backdrop for Main Street in Hills features several poles in the image, but I wanted at least one three-dimensional version for the foreground. Fortunately I've been able to develop a method for building utility poles that is both effective and economical, and allows me to quickly construct dozens in a single setting.

1. I started with some bamboo kabob skewers purchased from my local grocery store. The skewers have the advantage of already being a natural material, so it's easy to simulate the rough texture of the prototype poles. All that's needed is a quick stain with a wash of acrylic burnt umber paint.

2. For the crossarms I used Rix Products' telephone pole version. With the crossarms still on the sprue I painted them with a metallic spray paint to highlight the insulators, then trimmed the arm to length as well as removing unneeded insulators.

3. I then used a microbrush to apply the same burnt umber wash on the arm itself. Once dry, I attached the arm to the pole using gap-filling CA.

4. Bar Mills transformers were painted with the same metallic paint I used on the crossarms. I referenced prototype photos for the number and placement of the transformers on each pole, then secured them to the poles with CA. While I'd love to add power lines and string the poles together, that becomes difficult to accomplish on an operating model railroad, since they interfere with operators reaching into a scene to uncouple cars or line switches.

Greening the scene

1

2

3

With every component in place, I started on final scenery construction. I prefer to use natural materials where possible, including Scenic Express SuperTrees and ballast made from limestone paver sand. A large stiff paint brush helped shape and form the ballast profile and keep it off the tops of the ties, **1**.

For the base layer I used the Farm Pasture Static Grass Blend, also from Scenic Express, which matches the ground color and texture I see in Iowa, **2**. Damp paper towels were used to mask off areas where I didn't want the static grass to go. The towels are ripped to give a random and more natural edge to the scenic materials, **3**.

With the base scenery complete, I began placing the buildings and bins in their final location, **1**. Because of the height of the bins, they weren't permanently secured to the layout so access could be maintained for future maintenance and repairs.

Scenic Express SuperTrees were flocked with Superleaf material and mounted on the layout, **2**. I prefer to use natural materials wherever possible to increase the life-like appearance of his layout.

After installing trees and other large foliage, I added weeds, scrub, and underbrush **3**. They're made from poly-fiber fill dusted with Woodland Scenics blended turf, stretched thin to avoid clumping. I worked the weeds around the base of the structures, under the trees, and along roads as needed, referencing prototype photos.

Each layer was secured to the layout with diluted matte medium and allowed to dry for 24 hours. Once complete, I ran an abrasive cleaner atop the track and made sure that there weren't errant grains of ballast stuck to the rails before calling the scene complete.

Setting the mood

IAIS 708 leads train ICSW-08 across Main Street in Hills, Iowa. Despite not being an online business on my layout, Hills Grain and Feed serves as an excellent scene setter for The Hills Line. One glance tells my visitors and operators what the purpose and mission of the entire railroad was, is, and will continue to be; to provide personalized service to the smaller companies ignored or forgotten by the larger rail networks. Ultimately you can't ask for more from any industry on any layout, rail served or not.

Bringing it on-line

As designed, it would not take much to turn Hills Grain and Feed into an active rail-served customer. Despite its somewhat compact size, the complex could easily serve as a significant traffic source on a variety of layouts, and could ultimately be adaptable to a large assortment of model railroad concepts, regardless of era, scale, and locale.

Working the elevator would involve a train setting out a short string of covered hoppers on the siding, with the first car spotted underneath the spout. The next crew through town could pull the now loaded cars, or you could model the loading process as a separate job. The complex is too small to require a dedicated switch crew, but a track mobile or other "critter locomotive" could be kept on site to allow the elevator employees to move cars on their own.

If you're looking for larger capacity, extending the length of the tracks or the number of bins is always an option. But for me most of the appeal of the prototype is the small-town flavor that the smaller size provides.

Bill of materials

Bar Mills Scale Model Works
2021 – Utility Pole Transformers

Bossen Implement
ST50602 – 1/64 Grain Bin Roof Auger Kit 60

Evergreen Scale Models
142 – .040" x .040" strip
211 – .040" rod

GC Laser
19038 – gas meter

Grain Belt Models (Iowa Scaled Engineering)
HO-BIN18N07-HILLS – 18-foot galvanized steel grain bin
HO-BINDECAL – grain bin decal set

JTT Scenery Products
97338 – double parking lot light
97425 – concrete block sheet

MicroMark
81477 – Nibbling Cutter
82131 – Plasticutter

Microscale Industries
MI-1 – Micro Set solution
MI-2 – Micro Sol solution

PanPastel
30079 – GreyScale Kit
30074 – Sketch & Tone Kit

Pikestuff
541-0004 – Pre-fab warehouse
541-1008 – Cap tiles
541-3001 – Downspouts, gutters, chimney & meter

Plastruct
90431 – safety cage w/2 ladders
90501 – 3/64" styrene angle
90533 – 1/8" styrene channel
90672 – styrene ladder

Rix Products
628-0031 – Rix telephone pole crossarms
628-0304 – corrugated 30-foot grain bin
628-0356 – grain bin top 15 degree
628-0358 – grain bin parts

Scenic Express
653-6122 – Spring Green Superleaf
653-6132 – Medium Green Superleaf
EX886C – Farm Pasture Blend
EX0214 – SuperTree Value Pack

Tamiya
87038 – Extra Thin Cement
87095 – White Putty

Testors
1233T – Flat Light Aircraft Gray
1260T – Dullcote

Tomar Industries
H-862 – HO scale RR crossing signal

Walthers
933-3096 – Valley Growers Association Steel Grain Elevator
933-3123 – Big Grain Storage Bin
933-3733 – Roof Details
933-4075 – Electrical Fixtures
933-4121 – Modern Concrete Grade Crossing

Woodland Scenics
FP178 – Poly Fiber Green
T1349 – Blended Turf Green Blend

Miscellaneous
.025" piano wire
.040" 4x8-foot styrene sheet
120-grit sandpaper
91 percent isopropyl alcohol
Artists foamboard
Bamboo kabob skewers
Burnt umber acrylic paint
Cyanoacrylate adhesive
Diluted matte medium
Foam paint brushes
India ink
Limestone paver sand
Metallic and primer spray paints
Microbrushes
Paper towels
Razor saw and miter box
White and yellow acrylic craft paint

CHAPTER TEN

Diamonds in the tracks

By Todd Hermann // Photos by the author unless otherwise noted

The trees and those weeds have grown a bit, but CQ tower, the LNE diamonds, and the four-track main are still intact in this HO scale scene. The LVRR motorcar shanty visible in Furler's image is gone, as is the outhouse perched over the banks of the river, but otherwise the LVRR infrastructure is largely unchanged. The Reading's station has been relocated. Its former location is now just a gravel lot with plenty of room for the tower operator to park his car.

WHAT'S IN THE PHOTO

1. Catasauqua (CQ) tower. Milepost 97 on the Lehigh Valley RR. Completed in 1900.
2. LV maintainer's sheds. The signal and track gangs that worked out of Catasauqua made use of several lineside structures.
3. Lineside poles – elevated to clear the Lehigh & New England right of way.
4. LNE Catasauqua Branch and bridge across the Lehigh River. LNE trackage ended immediately after the diamonds crossing the LV.
5. LNE westbound upper-quadrant semaphore signal. Mounted on the Lehigh River bridge girders until the interlocking was rebuilt in 1958.
6. Former site of the LV's Catasauqua passenger station. After the station was removed in 1941, signal maintainers and track gangs used the site for storage.
7. Lehigh Valley main line. To the left, tracks continued to Lehighton, Pa., and ultimately Buffalo, N.Y. To the right, the line heads for Allentown, Pa., and eventually Jersey City, N.J.
8. Dwarf semaphore signal and switch for the LV's Track 6, which led to Biery Yard where interchange was conducted with the LNE and the Ironton Railroad, a cement-hauling short line that the Reading and LV owned jointly.
9. Catasauqua Station, Reading Co. Painted in the line's standard buff and brown colors, this was the stub-end terminus for the Reading's Catasauqua & Fogelsville Branch. The station was gone in my modeled era.
10. LNE's Catasauqua Job. Powered (in the prototype photo) on this day by nos. 613 and 612, a pair of Alco S-2s that were delivered from Schenectady in 1948.
11. Eastbound upper-quadrant semaphore signal. Hiding in the bushes, the signal and accompanying derail were controlled by the LV operator at CQ, but it sat on Reading Co. property.

Donald W. Furler specialized in action shots of steam locomotives, so the photograph featured here stands out a bit from the rest of his impressive body of work. It captures the overall scene and the unique physical plant more than any intense action. *Donald W. Furler – Center for Railroad Photography & Art Collection*

Located along the Lehigh River just a few miles north of Allentown, Pa., the small industrial town of Catasauqua and its immediate environs featured five different railroads in the mid-20th century: the Lehigh & New England, Central of New Jersey, Lehigh Valley, Reading, and the cement-hauling shortline Ironton RR. With multiple rail lines, a high volume of traffic, interesting physical plant, and busy interchange operations all packed into just couple miles of railroad, Catasauqua fascinated me from the first time I learned about it. That interest took me on a journey that led me to build my current layout as tribute to the area and the Lehigh & New England's Catasauqua Branch in particular circa the summer of 1956.

Those same factors are no doubt what drew the master photographer Donald W. Furler to set up his camera in West Catasauqua, just across the Lehigh River from the borough of Catasauqua proper, on multiple occasions in the late 1940s.

I've often wondered if Mr. Furler wished he had come just a few months earlier to record the last days of the LNE's 0-6-0 switchers that were assigned to this job prior to the arrival of diesel power. Instead, positioned on the Pine Street Bridge overlooking the scene on May 21, 1949, he "settled" for a pair of nearly new LNE Alco S-2s as they negotiated the signature feature of the local rail scene: the impossibly sharp, 46-degree curved crossing of the Lehigh Valley main line. It is passing the Reading Co.'s Catasauqua station and freight agency and is about to head eastward across the LV's four-track main line and the LNE's Lehigh River bridge. Once the Alcos begin to cross the LV diamonds, they will leave Reading Co. trackage and be back on home rails as they screech around the curve, bang over the diamonds and trundle across the LNE's Lehigh River bridge. Based on the location of their caboose, they might just be drilling the yard trackage behind the photographer. Or they could be headed back over to the east of side of the river to switch some of the LNE's consignees in Catasauqua itself.

Once their work is completed and they've collected the interchange traffic off the Reading, Ironton, LV and CNJ, they will make the 10-mile trip back their home base, the LNE yard at Tadmor near Nazareth, Pa. It was a cycle that repeated multiple times a day until the LNE called it quits at the end of October 1961. I'm too young have witnessed it, but as soon as I saw images from this area as a teenager, I knew I wanted to model it.

Planning the scene

1

1. The track configuration at West Catasauqua is unconventional and that's part of the appeal. A sharply curved crossing of a four track main line is unusual, but it also offered some helpful opportunities as I tried to fit this unique prototype scene into the confines of my basement as part an HO scale layout that features operations on the LNE's Catasauqua Branch as the centerpiece. The layout is walkaround-style with the LNE branch essentially serving as the "main line" that operators follow as they go. The sharp curve at West Catasauqua was a "must have" and I knew I wanted to create a scene that reproduced it as faithfully as possible. As modelers we tend to frown on sharp curves, but early on in the planning process I realized I could also use the curve to my advantage in the layout design. I could essentially use it to complete a turnback loop in the plan in a way that matched the look of the prototype scene.

2. In my plan, as the LNE branch travels west it goes under my basement stairs and makes a curve into what was once the closet beneath the staircase. Most of the approximately. 22"-radius curve directly beneath the stair treads is hidden trackage. This first curve under the stairs doesn't exist on the prototype, but it allows me to set up the approach for the West Catasauqua scene. After making that first turn, the line reemerges into a scenicked area, depicting the LNE's Lehigh River Bridge at Catasauqua. The right of way then executes a sharp curve to the right as it crosses the Lehigh Valley mainline, just as it did in reality.

I'm a paper and pencil planner. It looked feasible as a 1"-scale drawing on paper, but I made sure to test the design at full scale by transferring the design to paper template laid out on the basement floor.

Doing that allowed me to adjust the proportions of the scene and fine tune the track arrangement. I wanted the scene to look "right," but also operate reliably, so I tested this mock-up carefully. I compared the look of the scene to photographs and even taped down some sections of flextrack onto the full-size paper template on the basement floor and hooked it to my old MRC Tech II powerpack so I could run a test train back and forth through the proposed curve. This time spent on my hands and knees was well worth it. The curve was tight—just like the real thing—but it lined up well with prototype photos and it operated effectively.

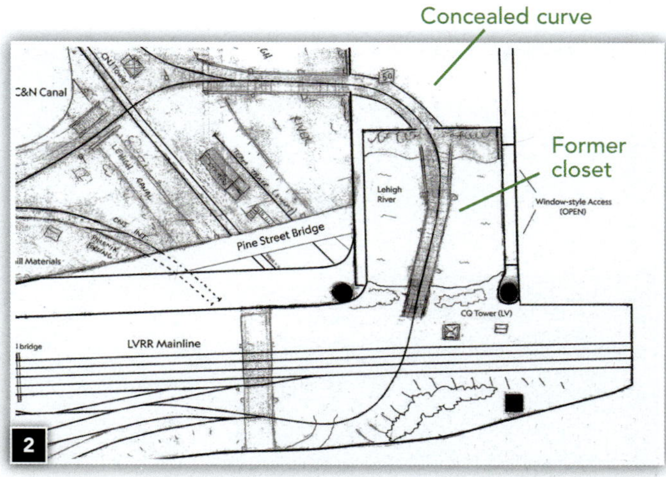

2

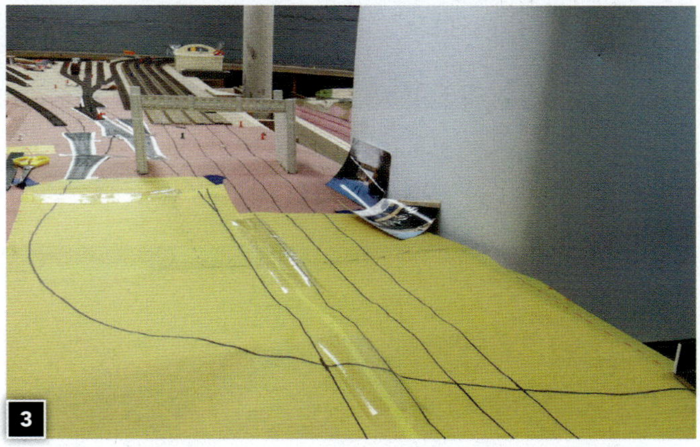
3

3. Once I was satisfied with the arrangement, I created an additional template of the track centerlines for the LV main and the LNE curve on yellow tracing paper. I knew that curve would need to be hand-laid—not an aspect of the hobby that I have much experience with, or honestly, much interest in.

I reached out to one of my mentors in the hobby, Scott Lefever, for advice on handlaying track. To my surprise, rather than just give me some advice, Scott volunteered to build the curved diamonds for me! Two other friends, Scott Ruth and Rob Quay, joined him in that effort during their round-robin layout work sessions. To guide their work, I sent them a copy of the full-size paper template of the track centerlines, some prototype photos, reference materials, and technical specs regarding rail size and tie length.

Prepping the space and building benchwork

While Scott, Rob, and Scott were building the curved diamonds, I pressed ahead with other aspects of the scene. Prepping the space and building benchwork came next.

The prospect of a long, narrow, deep scene extending back some 4 feet through the door opening of the old closet seemed like a recipe for trouble, so I decided to "daylight" the closet to improve access and more fully incorporate it into the walk-around style of the layout design. I removed the closet door and hardware, allowing me to look across the Lehigh River from West Catasauqua and back toward the east side of the river and Catasauqua itself. To enhance access and add another viewing angle, I framed in a 19x25-inch window into the wall of the closet that faced the aisle.

Doing that created a cool "shadow box" effect and allows operators to view the river bridge and the diamonds from another angle. Without that viewpoint and the reach-in access to the track it affords, the scene in the closet would be too deep to easily maintain, and even tougher for operators and visitors to fully appreciate.

For benchwork, I leaned heavily on the classic L-girder style of construction I learned while working in Scott and his wife, Judy's, hobby shops as a teenager. In the old closet space, where the Lehigh River bridge would be located, I attached L-girders to the stud walls on each side. This made it easy to add 1x4 joists to support the riverbed, track risers, and scenery.

Before working on the scene in the closet, I painted the backdrops. To paint my backdrops, shown here under construction in another part of the basement, I use two colors of flat latex wall paint from my local home improvement store: "Wild Blue Yonder" and "Ice White," both from Glidden/PPG. Working in 3- or 4-foot-long sections, I apply the darker sky blue to the top three quarters of the backdrop and the lighter ice white to the bottom using a roller. While they are still wet, I use a large flat brush to blend them together at the boundary line, which approximates the hazy sky that's common during summers in eastern Pennsylvania.

Installing the diamonds

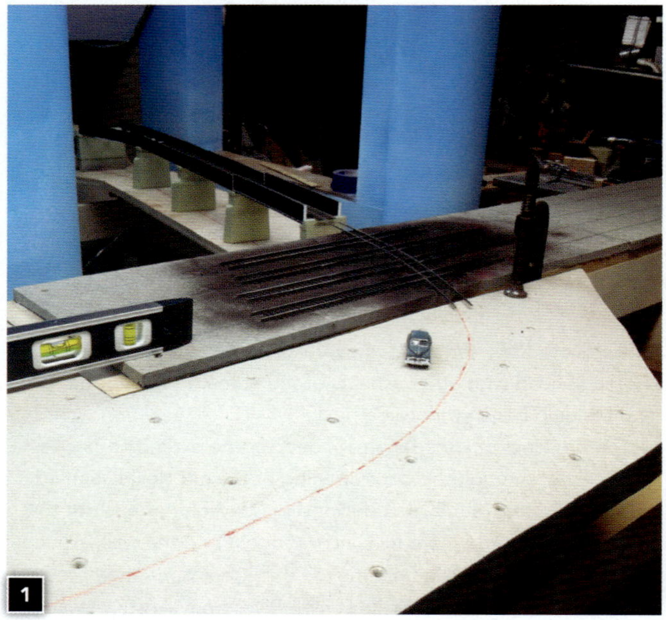

1

While all this was going on, Scott, Rob and Scott continued their work on the crossing. It wasn't long before another close friend and former hobby shop comrade, David Schwartz, arrived at my house to deliver the trackage. It was a team effort, to be sure!

The module matched my layout benchwork well and it fit right into the spot I'd reserved for it. The guys built a frame of 1 x 4s topped with high quality ¾" plywood subroadbed and Homasote sheet glued to that. It was perfect match for the construction I was using elsewhere on the railroad. The handlaid curve, diamonds, and the stub ends of the four LV mainline tracks are laid on wood ties with Shinohara Code 83 rail spiked directly in the Homasote. I wasted little time getting it installed, taking extra care to make sure it was plumb and level. And, of course, I spent time confirming that the overall look and feel of the trackage matched up with the prototype pictures that were guiding me. The track connecting to the handlaid portion is Micro-Engineering code 83 flextrack.

2

Scott Lefever and I had corresponded a few times during the building process about how the trackage would be wired. Scott and company suggested an old-school method. They cut gaps in the diamonds and filled them with styrene and epoxy. Then they wired up all four diamonds so the polarity of the crossing could be reversed to align correctly for a train on either the LNE branch or the LV main line with the flip of a single toggle switch. As of this writing, that old-school wiring approach has served me quite well. At some point in the future I plan to add a small desk with the operator's control for the Lehigh Valley's tower and this switch will be part of that set-up—hopefully connected to the operation of the semaphore signals.

LNE Lehigh River Bridge:

1

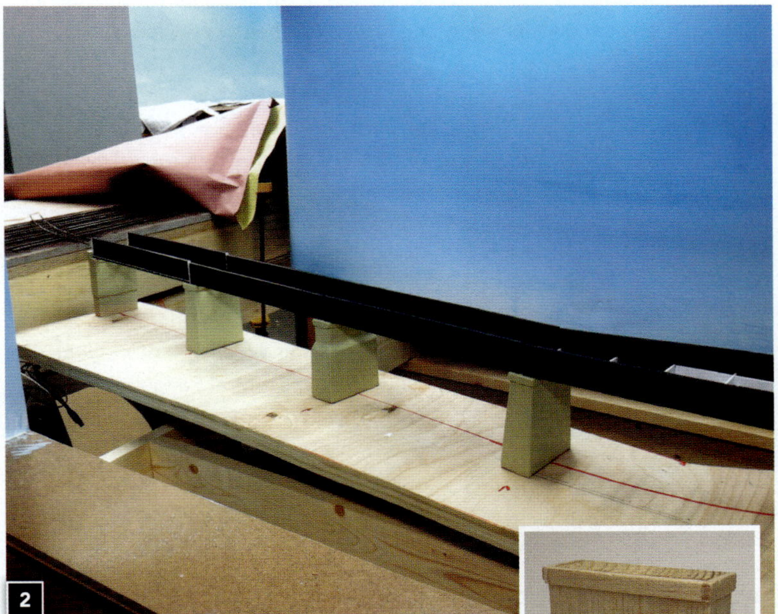

2

3

1. The LNE's plate girder span across the Lehigh River was built in 1904, replacing a Civil War-era covered bridge that served both rail and road traffic. It is one of the only structures in Furler's 1949 picture that still stands as of this writing in 2021. To re-create it in HO scale, I kitbashed four Central Valley Model Works' 72-foot-long plate-girder bridge kits. The CVMW bridge girders have rounded ends, The LNE bridge girders have squared ends, so I cut the rounded ends off the CVMW girders using a razor saw and built new, flat end plates with styrene.

2. In studying the photos, I noticed that the easternmost span (the one closest to the LV diamonds) features girders which are slightly taller than the other three sections of the bridge. To depict this, I increased the height of the Central Valley girders on this span a scale 6" by building up the bottom of the girder using strip styrene before gluing on the top and bottom rivet plates that come with the kit. The eastern end of the bridge, on the right in the photo, was widened to accommodate the curve of the track, but it also mimics the look of the actual bridge, which was wider on the east side of the river to accommodate a turnout on the bridge that led to a scrap yard.

When complete, I spray-painted the bridge flat black. Based on 8mm movie footage from the time period, we know that the LNE repainted the bridge in the mid-1950s, so I only lightly weathered it using a light washes of gray and rust-colored acrylic paint and AIM weathering powders.

3. The bridge abutments and piers were scratchbuilt around 1x3 wood block cores I carefully cut to the same height using a chopsaw (inset photo). Using wood cores ensured that the piers would be the same height and that the bridge (and its trackage) would be sitting on a solid foundation. The sloped sides of the piers and details like the cap sills and angled ice-breaks on the upstream side were added with balsa sheet and basswood strips.

I spread a thin layer of DAP PlasticWood "Natural" wood filler over the wood substructure using a putty knife. It doesn't need to look good at this stage. The goal is to cover all exposed surfaces that will be covered in "concrete" with a light coat of the wood filler. When I built the span, I was under the impression that the stone piers were parged with concrete to protect and strengthen them. There are signs of concrete parging on some of the piers today, but I've since concluded that the parging was mostly done for repairs and reinforcement in certain spots, so piers made of mostly of stone would have been more accurate. If I were to do it over, I'd build them to represent stone masonry construction.

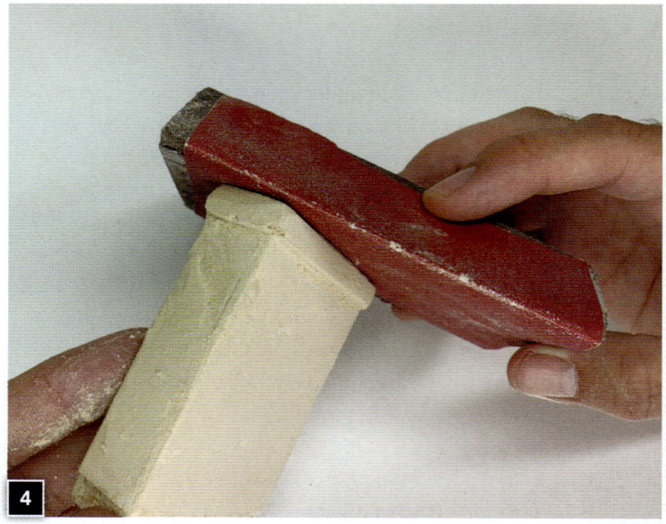

4

Once the filler dried overnight, I sanded it smooth with 150 grit sandpaper. This can be messy work; it is best done outdoors or away from the layout. The best part is that unless you are modeling a newly built structure it doesn't have to be perfect; the irregularities in the finish of the filler nicely simulate the look of aging concrete. PlasticWood can be carved, allowing you to add additional cracks and crumbling spots for even more weathering.

5

I sprayed the piers with a tan color from Rust-Oleum called Fossil. I followed that with a spray of Testor's Dullcote. When the spray dried, I painted on a blend of 60/40 blend MicroLux Aged Concrete, FolkArt Antique White acrylic paint, and water. I weathered them with light washes of Apple Barrel Pavement craft paint and various gray and brown weathering powders.

6

7

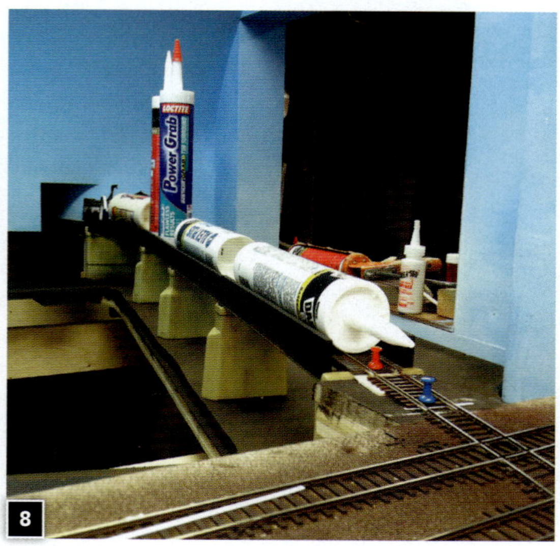

8

6. Once I finalized the position of the bridge, I painted the Gatorboard riverbed with a pair of murky brownish green colors from Glidden/PPG: Bronzed Ivy and Olive Black. I like Bronzed Ivy so much I now use it as the base color for all my scenery, both in the river and on land. After I added ground cover and scenery, I painted the river surface with gloss Mod Podge to simulate the river water. This part of the Lehigh River is relatively shallow and features some small rapids and eddies, so the Mod Podge nicely captures the look of flowing water.

7. With the river painted, I glued the piers to the Gatorboard riverbed using my favorite all-around adhesive: Zap Formula "560" Canopy Glue. This structure does not feature large, modern bridge shoes. I made smaller ones from Tichy Train Group Small Rivet Plates no. 8214. The bridge spans were also glued on with Canopy Glue.

8. The track was next. I used Micro-Engineering code 83 bridge flextrack to ensure a smooth transition to the code 83 diamonds. I pre-painted and weathered the track before installing it since it would be very difficult to do after it was in place. I attached the track with small amounts of DAP Clear Kitchen and Bath Adhesive caulk and held it down with a variety of ad-hoc weights until it set up.

Lehigh Valley tower and related structures

CQ Tower stood guard over the West Catasauqua diamonds from 1900 until 1958. I used a Lehigh Valley Standard Tower kit from Railway Heritage Models that is sold exclusively by the Anthracite Railroads Historical Society (anthraciterailroads.org/) as the starting point for my model. While the Lehigh Valley's two-story wood towers shared similar looks and features, many of them deviate from the "standard" version depicted in the kit. The placement of windows, doors, stairs, and other details vary. *John Gabriel*

I relocated the shed addition to the far side of the tower. Doing so was simply a matter of reversing the left and right sides of the building as I built the kit. Switching sides places the shed in the correct place, but as Furler's photo shows, there was no door on the side of the tower closest to the LNE tracks. Rather than try to fill in the door opening, I carefully cut out that section and replaced it with wood clapboard siding from Northeastern Scale Lumber (1⁄16" Scribed Siding).

The arrangement of the stairs to the upper level don't match CQ, but revising them is not difficult. To accomplish this, some parts, like the stairway landing platforms, need to be installed upside down or backward, but it's not noticeable. Slightly more significant surgery was needed on the rear of the tower's second floor. I added two additional windows on the back wall of the tower's second level to match the prototype. I cut a new opening for the middle window and I modified the original second story door opening to accommodate the corner window. I also relocated the door.

In its final decade of active service, the tower also featured a very narrow two-story addition with a small window. This was added in 1949 to house a small CTC machine that controlled the interlocking up the line at Cementon, Pa., where the LV mainline had been reduced from four tracks to two in an early bid to cut costs and boost efficiency.

Lacking plans, I had to estimate the dimensions and ended up building this odd-looking little addition using more of the Northeastern Scale Lumber 1/16" clapboard siding with trim made using Midwest Products scale lumber. The small window was salvaged from my parts bin, as was the roof. The addition replaces one of the original windows on the tower, so I was able to re-use those parts to make the extra windows on the back of the tower. I was able to cobble together the last window in the back using some other unused detail parts and excess laser-cut wood "sprue" from this highly versatile kit.

I followed the kit instructions and pre-painted the parts before assembly using an airbrush. Lehigh Valley lineside structures featured a two-tone dark and light gray color scheme. I used Model Master 2079 Schwarzgrau for the trim and Model Master 1740 Dark Gull Gray for the siding. The roof was painted Scalecoat Flat Grimy Black. The caps on the roof peaks are MicroLux Roof Brown. The tower's awnings are also Model Master Dark Gull Gray. By the mid-1950s the tower's exterior was showing its age. To represent the faded look, I applied thinned washes of the Model Master colors by hand, varying the shades on individual boards to add to the weathered look.

LV maintainer's shanty

Just beyond the tower in Furler's picture you can see the largest of the track and signal maintainer's shanties at Catasauqua. Lacking plans I relied on photos and measurements from Sanborn Fire Insurance maps to estimate the proportions for this structure and the smaller shed that sat beside it. I built paper and cardstock mock-ups to test the size of the buildings. Since the larger shed featured a hip roof, the paper template was also a useful guide for cutting those parts for the final structure.

I scratchbuilt this structure using Northeastern Scale Lumber 1/16" clapboard, Midwest Products scale lumber, and windows and doors from Tichy and a few salvaged from an AM Models yard office kit. The distinctive finials on the roof were made with styrene rod and small beads from my wife's stash of jewelry-making supplies.

Other details

Lineside Poles: These are made using Rix Products pole kits. The poles that allow the wires to clear the LNE right of way were very tall. To get the right height I glued an extra section of pole to bottom on the poles on either side of the LNE. I added woodgrain texture with the blade of an old Atlas Snap Saw. Then I spray-painted them Rust-Oleum Camo Brown and hand-painted the insulators NYC Jade Green and gave everything several washes of light gray craft paint for weathering.

Signal boxes: Various types are available from Details West and others, but to better match the look of the prototype, I scratchbuilt mine from Evergreen styrene strip and brass wire.

Interlocking plant details

1. CQ tower controlled a rod-and-lever armstrong-style interlocking plant. I built mine using the techniques described in a chapter by Bill Darnaby that was included in the Kalmbach book *The Model Railroader's Guide to Junctions* by Jeff Wilson, and in the January 2004 issue of *Model Railroader*.

I followed Bill's methods for creating the rods and carriers with some modifications. At Catasauqua, the Lehigh Valley used extra-long crossties as the anchor points for the interlocking rod-and-lever hardware. Using photos as my guide, I glued extensions to the ties using extra ties from Micro-Engineering flextrack.

2. I used 3-foot lengths of .015"-diameter K&S no. 498 music wire for the rods and 4x4 brass mesh from Eduard (part 00101), a Czech military model kit manufacturer, to make the carriers that held the rods along the right of way. Following Bill's example, I cut out the carriers from the mesh to accommodate the correct number of rods, then glued them to footers made of small pieces of .030" styrene using cynaoacrylate adhesive (CA).

To create a stronger bond and help the carriers remain upright when being glued, I used a razor saw to carve a shallow groove into each styrene piece and placed the mesh in the groove. These represent the carrier hardware that was attached to the elongated ties. The flat styrene surface also makes it easier to glue the assembly to the ties when the time comes.

After mass producing all the carriers I would need, I threaded the piano wire into them, but I did not glue them to the rods yet. Keeping the piano wire organized during this process required a good deal of patience and space.

The K&S wire comes in 3-foot lengths, but the scene on the layout is a about 4 feet long in total and there are varying numbers of rods in the carriers across the interlocking, so I divided the project into several assemblies to complete the scene. With rods threaded on the carriers at the workbench (but not glued in place), I carefully moved each assembly to the layout and finalized the placement of the carriers to ensure they matched the location of the ties.

3. Once I was happy with their placement, I used a small amount of CA to bond the wire rods to the brass mesh in the carriers. Importantly, I still did not attach them to the ties at this point. Instead, I carefully transferred the assemblies to the paint booth and sprayed them with a 50/50 Grimy Black/Roof Brown mix. After I painted and ballasted the track in this area, I installed the rod assemblies with CA, working slowly and carefully down the line to ensure the rods were lined up as straight as possible.

1

2

3

Tower foundation and walkways

Adding a foundation was another key part of the tower construction process.

I used balsa to make a foundation that matched the building's footprint. I glued the balsa directly to the Homasote with yellow carpenter's glue and brush painted it with Aged Concrete from MicroLux.

After I added cinders and ballast around the foundation, I built the wooden walkway from the stairs to the tracks by cutting individual 2x6 boards out of Midwest Products Scale Lumber no. 8003 using my NorthWest Short Line Chopper II.

I stained the individual boards with Minwax "Early American" stain. After that dried, I glued the boards to a backing strip of .020" styrene using canopy glue to create the walkway configuration I wanted. I installed footers on them using additional pieces of stripwood. Also shown is the wooden shroud over the rocking bar assembly at the foot of the tower.

1

2

Semaphores

1. I built the signals protecting the LNE crossing using upper-quadrant signal parts from Tomar Industries. Tomar's brass parts have some over-sized elements, but they are quite versatile and produce good-looking, durable signals that automate well. Using photos to guide me, I cut the parts to size, soldered them together and painted them. They will be controlled using Tam Valley Depot servos and their 3-Way Signal Driver board.

The hardware cabinet was scratchbuilt with styrene. The eastbound derail that was interlocked with the signal is visible on the other side of the tracks. I built it as a static model made with an extra section of rail, styrene strip, and rail brace detail parts from Details West (RB-920).

2. One distinctive feature of the scene at West Catasauqua is the semaphore mounted atop the girder of the LNE's Lehigh River bridge.

In addition to cutting down the signal's mount so it was narrow enough to sit on the girder, I also fashioned an extra-long actuating wire to control the signal. It runs through a hole in the bridge and down through another hole in the river bank to connect with the servo under the benchwork.

With the addition of some more foliage under the bridge, the wire is not noticeable. One advantage to using ¾" plywood as a base for the trackwork—even beneath this river bridge—is that you always have a solid place to mount any needed hardware, like the servos, below decks.

West Catasauqua scenery

I built the riverbanks and the hill in West Catasauqua using layers of extruded-foam insulation board and green florist foam. Use of the latter is a technique I first learned about from Mike Confalone and his Allagash Railway. As much as possible, I place florist foam in locations likely to be forested, since it does such an excellent job of holding trees in place without adhesive. The less expensive insulation board is used elsewhere. After roughing out the shape, I carved the hillside to approximate height and contour based on photographs. In this case it took me several evenings of "foam editing" to get it how I wanted it.

Ground cover

I cover the non-rocky areas of the landscape that need additional gap-filling or texture with a simplified version of Lou Sassi's tried and true "Ground Goop" mixture (see the recipe in Chapter 12).

Even if you are modeling summer, I've found it very helpful to refer to photographs of the area you are modeling during the winter. The lack of foliage on the trees allows you to get a better sense of the underlying topography, including the locations of another significant scenic feature at West Catasauqua: rock outcrops.

Paving the access road

Curiously, the road that led to the Reading's C&F station only appears to have been paved after the station had been moved to another location. It was paved in my modeling time frame, so that was my next task.

The road features a paved grade crossing, then slopes upward on a curving path and ends at the fascia. I paved it using DAP Patch-n-Paint spackle from the local hardware store that I tinted with a few drops of black acrylic craft paint. When mixed, a few drops is enough to the turn the filler gray without noticeably affecting its ability to dry and cure.

I used sections of N scale cork roadbed to create forms along the sides of the road and made sure to extend those forms across the tracks since they'd be covered as a grade crossing. One thing I wish I had done was cut a piece of thin (.020") styrene to cover the ties both between and outside the rail under the grade crossing. This would prevent the spackle from sagging into the gaps between the ties as it dries, creating an unwanted washboard effect.

I find road paving to be an easy and relatively forgiving process using spackle. First, place several dollops of tinted spackle into the roadbed, between the forms—enough to fill it when it's been flattened out. Using too much here is preferable to not enough.

If you have a putty knife that's wide enough to reach the forms on either side of the road you can use it as a screed to smooth out the material and "pave" the road. Pressing the screed against the forms as you smooth out the paving material ensures the sides stay level and it help create a flat, even surface. Over the course of layout construction I've made several screeds of different widths using straight-edged pieces of .060" styrene left over from making my backdrops.

Before it dried, I cleared the flangeways at the grade crossing using a set of plastic-wheeled Athearn freight car trucks I keep on hand for just this job.

Lehigh Valley station/ MOW depot site

The Lehigh Valley station site sat directly across the LVRR main from the Reading's. Just the like the Reading's, this is an abandoned station in my time period. The LV tore down its Catasauqua station in the fall of 1941, but the foundation, station platforms, and the retaining walls that elevated it above the Lehigh River were still quite visible in 1956.

Maintenance-of-way crews used the station's concrete platforms to store rail and other equipment. I roughed in the station area using Homasote and insulation board. I built the concrete retaining walls (which also still stand as of 2021) using the same technique I used on the LNE bridge piers: a balsa and basswood frame with a sanded coat of DAP Plastic Wood filler to simulate concrete.

The old station platforms are made of sheet styrene that I scribed with lines to represent the joints in sidewalk-style poured concrete. I used strip styrene to represent the foundation walls. As a reference, I used a 1953 aerial photo print of the area in my collection which, along with Donald Furler photograph, and 8mm movie footage from John Pechulis Media DVDs show the platforms, station foundation shape, and other details quite well.

Dirt, cinders, and ballast

I used a mix of black art sand (cinders) and Scenic Express medium dirt as the base ground cover on the station site. The area between the platforms and the LV main line is all cinders, but I added progressively more dirt to the mix when I filled in the area where the station once stood.

I glued it down using 70 percent alcohol to "wet" the surface without disturbing the arrangement of rocks and dirt, then a white glue-water-alcohol mix applied with a pipette for control. While the whole area is still wet you can go back and sprinkle in more cinder and dirt as needed to fill bare spots or add accents.

Looking back

Donald Furler captured the scene circa 1949, but I model the mid-1950s after dieselization was complete on all the local railroads and, in the words of Catasauqua rail historian Joe Yurko, after "the weeds started to grow" on the property and the fortunes of the area's rail lines started to wane. Fortunately, another accomplished Allentown-area rail photographer named Ken von Steuben also had the presence of mind to capture the scene from the rear vestibule of Lehigh Valley No. 9, the westbound *Black Diamond*, just after it banged across the steel diamonds at West Catasauqua in June 1957—just one summer after the year I'm depicting.

Looking back toward Allentown, a semaphore signal bridge is visible at the east end of the interlocking. That structure and its signals along with its partner at the other end of the interlocking will be replaced in 1958 with target-style signals on lineside masts. On the right, the dwarf semaphore still protects the switch to Track 6, the lead for the LV's Biery yard where interchange with the LNE and Ironton was handled.

For me, it's always interesting to hear what inspired other modelers' interest in a particular railroad. Some of us are drawn to what is familiar or reminds us of a hometown or a favorite railfan spot. For others, there's a powerful lure in modeling something that we don't see everyday—the unfamiliarity of a railroad and its unique visual setting pulls us in. For some, it's a chance to re-create a time or place that has changed dramatically or a railroad that no longer exists. For me, it's combination of factors. I hope I've conveyed that here.

Ken von Steuben, Mike Bednar collection

CHAPTER ELEVEN

Building from inside out

By Ron Hoess // Photos by the author unless otherwise noted

My layout depicts a portion of the Pennsylvania Railroad's Chestnut Hill Branch, an electrified commuter line that ran from North Philadelphia to the northern outskirts of the city. The first 2 miles of the Chestnut Hill Branch, where it leaves the PRR main line in North Philadelphia, was heavily industrialized. Among the major industries served were the Budd Company, Midvale Steel, and Philco, which generated an extraordinary amount of freight traffic along this commuter line.

While the Budd Co. is most often associated with manufacturing railcars, a major portion of its business was the production of automobile body parts. By the late 1950s, the time period I am modeling, railcar manufacturing had been moved to another plant in Northeast Philadelphia, and the Hunting Park Plant along the Chestnut Hill Branch focused primarily on producing auto body parts.

The prototype photograph typifies this production with workers loading automobile doors and hoods into waiting

Workers at the Budd Plant at Hunting Park Avenue in Philadelphia load stamped automobile hoods and doors. *Dick Foley collection*

Ron Hoess's HO scale model of the Budd Plant in the Hunting Park section of Philadelphia has an interior loading dock, just like the prototype.

WHAT'S IN THE PHOTO

1. 50-foot auto parts boxcar
2. Auto door assembly
3. Auto hood assembly
4. Conveyor chain
5. Conveyor hooks
6. Racks for carrying parts
7. Warren trusses and overhead lights
8. Overhead conveyor for transporting automobile parts
9. Automobile parts including doors, door panels and hoods
10. Carts with stacked automobile parts waiting to be loaded into boxcars
11. Office for coordinating shipments
12. Forklift for moving automobile parts

boxcars. Two noteworthy features are the loading dock itself being inside the building, and the auto parts being delivered to the loading dock by an overhead conveyor belt.

Judging from the shape of the car doors and hoods, the photograph was probably taken in the late 1940s or early 1950s. While this photograph was the primary motivation for building the model, I have relied on additional photographs, including recent ones taken in the now abandoned plant, to help with such details as color and structure.

Since the Chestnut Hill Branch is electrified with overhead catenary, all sidings for switching on the layout are placed in front of the catenary to avoid having operators reaching over the delicate wires. As a result, my sidings for the Budd plant are at the edge of the layout. This was an unforeseen plus since it meant I could have the sidings enter a building with the fascia side of the building open for viewing.

Since the structure was going to have considerable interior detail, I started from the inside and worked outward.

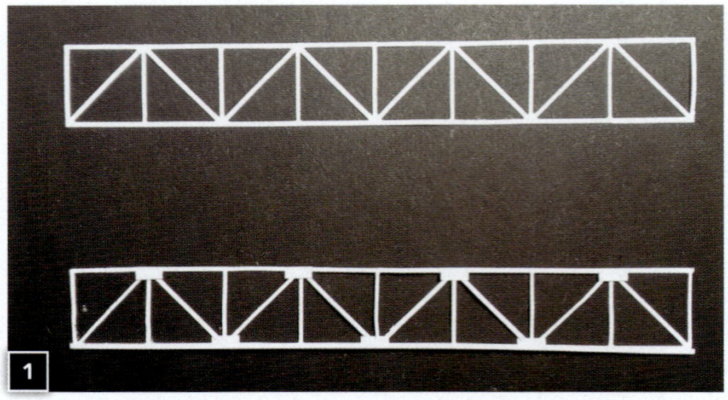

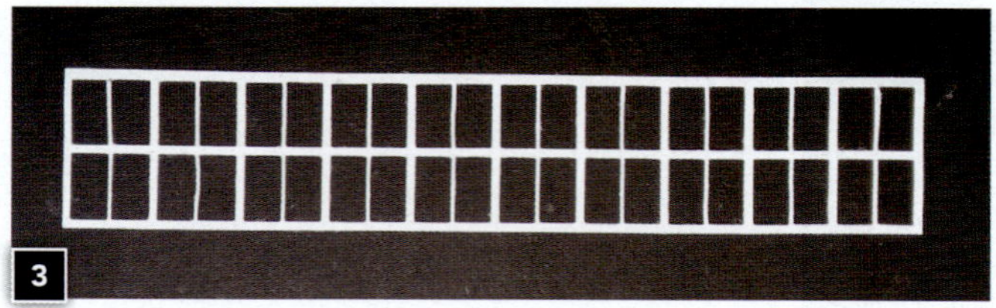

1. When I started building this structure in the summer of 2016, I had just purchased a Cameo Silhouette Craft Cutter and was anxious to see how useful it would be in scratchbuilding structures.

Careful inspection of a number of Budd Co. interior photographs indicated the roof was supported by Warren trusses. Using the digital cutter software, I designed the Warren trusses to connect each set of two vertical H-columns and then proceeded to cut them from heavy cardstock. At the time, I was concerned the cardstock might not be rigid enough, so I added a strip of .040"-square Evergreen strip styrene to the bottom horizontal beam to act as a stiffener. In addition, gusset plates of .100" × .010" strip styrene were added to each of the joints.

2. The Warren trusses were then glued between the two sets of H-columns. More H-columns that would serve as the base for the roof were then glued horizontally on top of the vertical H-columns. To represent electrical conduit, two .040" rods (Evergreen 211) were glued to the tops of the Warren trusses and run the length of the structure. To each of these horizontal rods, seven vertical rods of .040" styrene were attached, each having a Tichy lamp reflector (no. 8027) glued to the end.

Before enclosing the interior portion of the structure, various parts needed to be painted. A number of recent interior photographs of the abandoned Budd buildings indicate the interior walls and columns were painted sky blue from the floor to a height of about 4 feet. Above the 4-foot level, everything was painted an off white color.

3. One feature that was characteristic of many of the Budd buildings was the use of a sawtooth roof, which was an efficient way to provide light for the interior. I designed the frame and mullions of the windows on my Cameo Silhouette and cut them from cardstock.

4. After painting they were glued to transparency film, which served as the window glazing. These were then combined with sheet styrene for the roof portion and corrugated metal siding (Evergreen 4526) to complete the roof assembly.

Since both the inside and outside walls of the building can be viewed, I made a sandwich of brick sheet (N-Scale Architect modern brick 50001) for the outside wall, a middle layer of plain .020" sheet styrene, and concrete block (N-Scale Architect concrete block 50005) for the inside wall. The wall that runs parallel to the tracks has a number of large industrial windows. These were custom laser-cut and were leftovers from another project but worked nicely here.

5. The glass for the windows again was cut from clear transparency sheets. Typically when modeling structures, the window glass is on the inside, but in this case the windows are going to be viewed from the inside of the structure so I reversed the order and put the window frame and mullions on the inside, which looked much better.

With the overall building structure assembled, I turned to the final details of the loading dock. The most challenging aspect was constructing the overhead conveyor system for transporting the auto parts to the loading dock. There are a number of photographs (see the Digital Hagley Archives) that show the overhead conveyor system that ran throughout the Budd plant to transport parts.

5

6

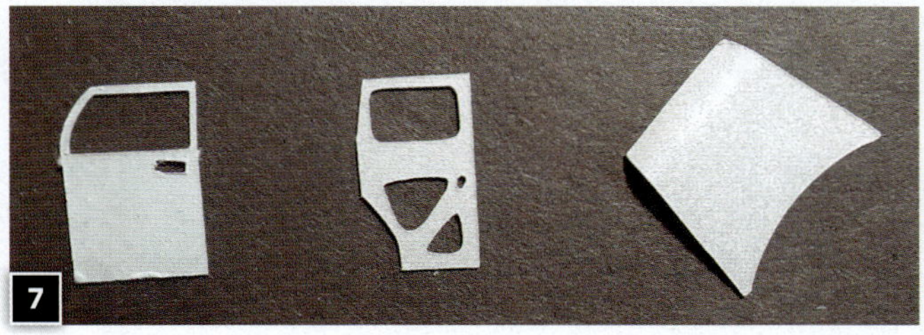

7

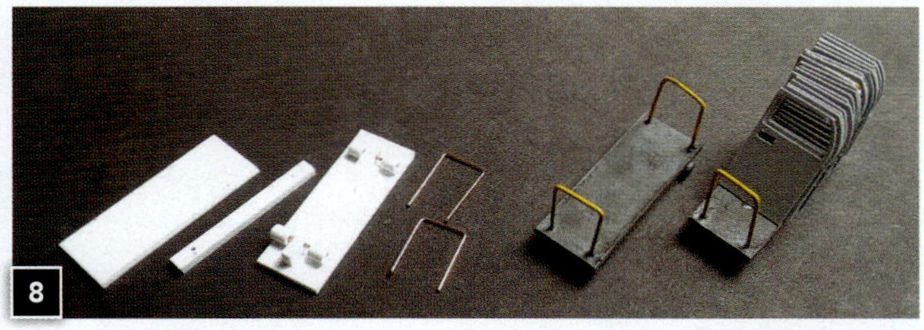

8

6. The conveyor had rollers spaced about every 3 feet held in a track. Each roller had a metal hook attached which went through a chain that was responsible for moving the rollers. Parts to be transported were then hung on the bottom of each hook. To model this I started with .060" styrene channel stock (Evergreen 262) in which I inserted small pieces of 3/64" styrene rod (Evergreen 221) spaced about 3 scale feet apart.

Each of the rod pieces was drilled to accept a piece of .010"-diameter phosphor bronze wire (Tichy 1101). The pieces of wire were then bent downward to form a hook from which the auto parts could be hung.

A critical element is a chain that must be threaded through each hook. I finally settled on an inexpensive necklace from WalMart. I suspended the conveyor from the roof structure using strip styrene so the hooks are about 12 scale feet from the loading dock floor.

7. Now it was time to start making auto parts to be sent to the loading dock. The first was a door panel I drew using the Cameo Silhouette cutter's software. To make sure it was sized correctly, I compared samples to HO scale vehicles on my layout. The doors were cut from cardstock craft paper that had a metallic silver color that nicely matched the Budd-produced parts. To add some variety I also found a picture of an interior door panel (See Hagley digital archives) and was able to produce that on the cutter as well.

Finally, some car hoods were needed. This presented a somewhat different problem, since in general, car hoods have a more three-dimensional character to them. Only after sacrificing and cutting up one of my plastic 1950s automobiles did I realize that by the late 1950s, car hoods had become almost flat with only a slight curvature in front.

This was perfect since I am modeling 1958 and Budd would be producing parts for that year or the next. After drawing and cutting the hood, I took each hood and carefully bent the front part of the hood over a 1/8" brass rod to give the necessary curvature. All of

9

these parts—doors, door panels, and hoods—could then be hung from the hooks on the conveyor.

8. While my 1940s photograph did not show carts loaded with auto parts, they appear in other photographs from Budd.

The base of each cart is made from .040" styrene measuring a scale 3x8 feet. On the underside I glued .060" x .100" strip styrene down the center line of the cart. At each end of the styrene strip, I drilled holes to accept .020"-diameter phosphor bronze wires (Tichy 1103) that serve as the axles for the wheels. The wheels are small pieces of 3/32" tubing (Evergreen 223) glued to the axles. I formed more .020" phosphor bronze wire into the handles at each end with a bending jig.

9. More than likely there was some central point, such as an office, that helped orchestrate the loading of auto parts into incoming freight cars.

To represent the theorized office, I constructed a small concrete block structure to match the internal walls of the overall structure and located it at the far end of the loading dock. The office is very simple, with a door and a small picture window overlooking the loading dock.

CHAPTER TWELVE

Harvey's HO scale model included some changes to the prototype arrangement to better fit his modeling space. For example, the model streetcars enter and exit the scene in the opposite direction of the prototype. On Harvey's model, the parking lots serve as "breathing space" as green landscapes would in a rural layout.

Sometimes your inspiration can come from Google Maps. Harvey Simon knew he wanted to complete his HO scale San Francisco F-line layout with a Fisherman's Wharf scene. Looking at the area on Google Maps helped Harvey decide how to lay out the scene. *Google Maps*

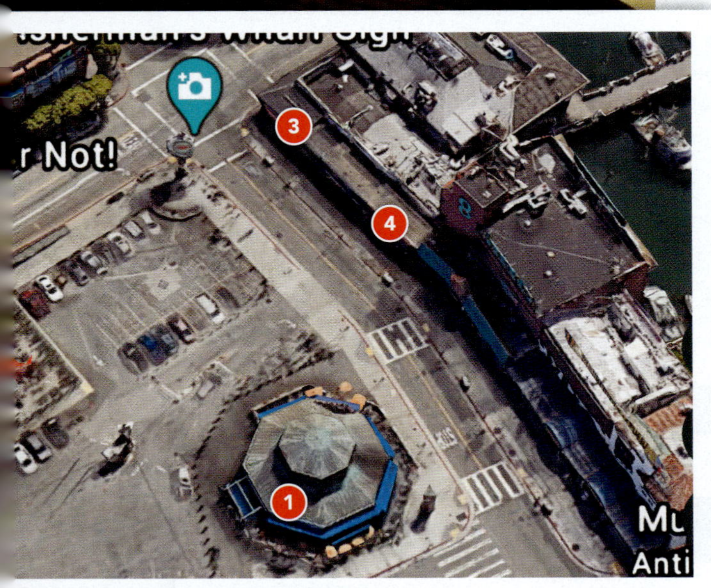

Building Fisherman's Wharf

By Harvey Simon // Photos by the author unless otherwise noted

After seven years building a 35-square-foot layout depicting San Francisco's F-line trolley system, the finish line was in sight. It's been a wonderful ride, and with the completion of Fisherman's Wharf, I could finally watch the trolleys make a complete run on a fully scenicked layout—starting in the Castro District, moving through the downtown area and arriving and turning around at Fisherman's Wharf (see *Great Model Railroads 2022* for more on the F-line).

Fisherman's Wharf is one of San Francisco's most famous areas and has many interesting attractions for tourists and residents. Millions of people visit Fisherman's Wharf annually, an area rich in sights and seafood. As I thought about capturing the area's flavor, I quickly discovered the tricky part in composing the scene was determining what buildings and other scenic elements would make the cut. So the goal became creating a convincing scene in which the various elements could be scaled down to the available space yet still look like everything belonged.

Google maps was a key research tool. Being able to take a virtual tour of the area, snapping street level screenshots along the way, helped me choose structures, while the satellite views provided the orientation. Like the other structures on my layout, each building represents a prototype. Many are rather ordinary, and ordinary is good, particularly those against the backdrop or layout edge. These include the Holiday Inn and Denny's (a kitbash using Design Preservation Models modular wall parts), strip center (a Summit CustomCuts backdrop flat kitbash), a block of three adjacent businesses—Latte Express, Aroma Tea, and bike rental shop (scratchbuilt using Magnuson wall remainders from other projects), and Crab Station and Gram's Lighthouse (scratchbuilt, also using old Magnuson parts). The other structures in the scene include Supreme Crab (scratchbuilt), Chowder Hut (3D printed) and the large Fisherman's Wharf sign (3D printed) that is a landmark in itself. To capture the waterfront, I scaled down an oldie-but-goodie—Campbell Scale Models wharf, no. 307.

WHAT'S IN THE PHOTO

1. Chowder Hut
2. Supreme Crab
3. Crab Station and
4. Gram's Lighthouse

1

Getting started

1. With the footprint established (more on that later) I added the backdrop, an actual photomural of the San Francisco skyline, and to gauge for scale, I placed the first structure. I thought everything looked fine, so I glued the backdrop in place. You'll note the blank space to the right of the building. I had hoped to find a scene extender that would better accommodate the road leading into the backdrop.

Interestingly, I thought I had the perfect solution while California was in lockdown during the pandemic. There were many street level photographs of a deserted San Francisco on the internet that I thought would work. Unfortunately, I wasn't able to size them properly, but the point of sharing this, is you often don't know where inspiration will come from. I teach part time, and as I tell my students—be observant and curious. Solutions to problems often come from unexpected sources.

Dave Simon

2

2. The first building as the orange Milan trolley no. 1893 enters the scene is what was then a Holiday Inn and Denny's. Since I began the project, the hotel has been renamed and painted. Here I took DPM modular wall components (now Woodland Scenics) and fashioned a reasonable replica of the prototype. The major modification is to the windows, and you can see the sequence of changes I made to get close to those of the actual building.

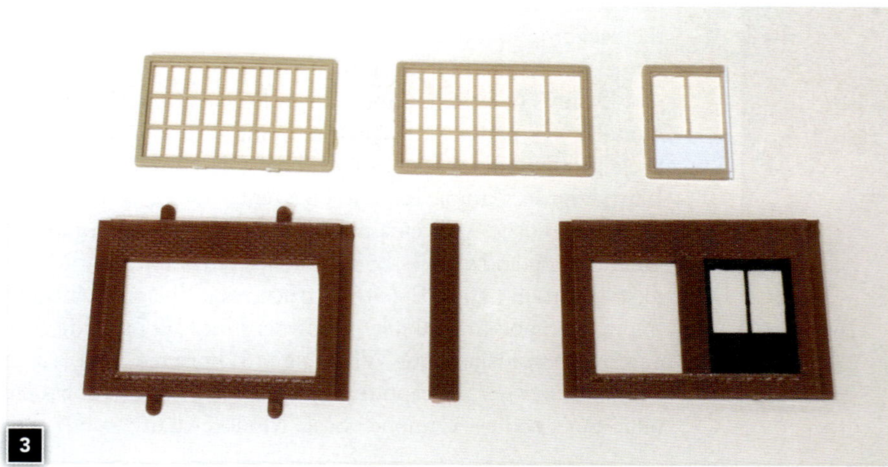

3

3. I started with DPM kits nos. 30174 and 30175 (two and one story sections), but then removed some mullions and shortened the window. Note how I used a pilaster to bisect the opening to create two windows. For the bottom of each window I added a cut-to-fit piece of clapboard styrene—Evergreen no. 4041. When painted black, the windows are a reasonable match to the prototype. There was a hedge row along the first floor partially blocking the parking garage. I used a JTT 95510 flower hedge row to model this. One other noteworthy detail—there are small lights above the three bays on the first floor. I modeled these using the tips of clear sprues from an earlier project. It's often a good idea to save everything as you never know when

Dave Simon

a stray part may come in handy. Note also how I have a car exiting the parking garage.

4

4. The next building is the block-long strip center. On the prototype there's a building between it and the Holiday Inn, but I only had room for one, so I chose this one. Summit Customcuts offers a backdrop flat (ML-002) that I used as the basis of the structure. Here, I made straightforward modifications that enabled me to get close to the prototype. I decided not to attempt the second story corner structure as there wasn't enough room for the roof against the backdrop, so I added the green panel instead. This panel is actually on the right side of the row of stores, but I brought it to the left side to counterbalance the awning from the Walthers Ashmore Hotel kit, which was remaining. My favorite store is the Segway rental shop. Here, I took a DPM dock door left from the Holiday Inn building, painted it gray, and then cut out and pasted the cool-looking Segway logo on the door. I was hoping to find HO scale Segway riders, but so far, no luck. I'll have to keep looking. One last point—note how I offset the strip center from the Holiday Inn, rather than a flush adjacency. Too often I see backdrop flats as one continuous run without a break. By offsetting the two structures there's more room for activity in front of the shopping center which I believe adds visual interest.

5

Dave Simon

5. Across the street from the prototype is the block of stores I built for the layout edge after the trolley rounds the corner from the strip center. Latte Express, Aroma Tea, and the bike rental shop are adjacent in real life and I chose these three as they fit the available space. I could simply have left them out, but these stores help frame the large parking lot, so I decided the extra effort to build them was worth it. Using screen shots from Google maps, I built the three shops as one unit using old Magnuson wall sections that were sitting in my "maybe-I'll-be-able-to-use-these-later" bin.

You'll note the storefront signage on all my buildings, and how it closely matches the prototypes. This is a critical element in telling the story. In an urban setting especially, where there are many structures, having prototypically correct signage differentiates the buildings the trolley passes along the run. Some signs, like the Segway logo, I was able to print off the internet; for others I called upon the same graphic artist who made the signs for the Castro district that worked so well. And depending on your enthusiasm for scratchbuilding and kitbashing, another benefit is you won't see these buildings on other layouts, adding to their authenticity.

1

Parking lot

1. The center of the scene is the Fisherman's Wharf parking lot. This was a fun build as it covers a lot of area and wasn't as time consuming as building structures. Since I had already laid track, the sidewalks were in place, making it easier to plaster the open space. I began by pouring pre-tinted patching plaster and then sanding it smooth. The satellite photos helped with color. I mixed the plaster with Woodland Scenics Stone Gray, then used this straight from the bottle to paint the parking lot. The challenging part is getting that mottled look, which I achieved through trial and error using different shades of gray and tan mixed with a little white to provide contrast. I added some chalk weathering in the same colors and randomly rubbed it in with my fingers. The idea is to create a variety of tones all blended together.

2

Dave Simon

Next I added the parking spaces. The spaces are 8 scale feet wide and 15 feet long. Here I used painters tape to provide masking in order to paint straight lines. I also added a handicapped space that's wider than a regular space. I had some old Polly Scale D&H Avon blue that worked fine for the lines, following which I added a handicapped symbol to the pavement. I got this from the internet, sanded the back very thin, and cemented in place. Sanding the back helps it look like it was painted on the asphalt.

Three other important details help enhance the parking lot. The first is

3

Dave Simon

1

Dave Simon

the chain link fence, which reflects the prototype. Here I went to YouTube for instruction, and found Luke Towan's excellent tutorial. Following his method, I was able to get reasonable results. Of course, like everything else in the hobby, by the time I made and installed the last section, I had gotten pretty good at making a chain link fence.

2. I also had fun building the gate house where cars enter the lot. I had taken a screen shot of the prototype, then, using Evergreen Styrene, built this little feature. Having the entry gate in the "up" position after the car enters the lot adds activity to the scene. You'll also note in the prototype photo the location of Supreme Crab, discussed in the next section.

3. The last detail is the pole sign. I had the graphic artist design the sign from a screen shot of the actual sign. I then traced the outline of the sign onto a scrap piece of Magnuson resin sidewalk from an old kit, cut it out using a Dremel scroll saw, and then cemented the sign in place.

Supreme Crab

1. Supreme Crab is a Cajun-style seafood restaurant that is located at the corner of the parking lot on Jefferson Street. Given its actual location—abutting the street and the parking lot—and what I thought was an interesting-looking building—I added it to the scene.

This structure wasn't part of my original thinking, but it serves the purpose of tying the parking lot to the buildings surrounding it. That it also has interesting architecture, like the overhang on the front wall, a neat-looking sign—I like that the "C" in Crab is a crab—and a giant "EAT CRAB" sign on the side of the building adds punch to the overall look. I also added interior lighting as the prototype has a series of large windows on the second floor where the restaurant actually is. There are other shops on the first floor, but I didn't have any entry doors in my remainders box, so I excluded them. I put generic backgrounds in the windows, but didn't identify the stores.

Here again, by studying the structure from the screen shots, I was able to get a reasonable facsimile of the actual building using basic materials—sheet styrene and strips cemented together. The large windows on the second floor—also built from strip styrene—provided a great opportunity for modeling and lighting the interior. The key ingredients include the Preiser table and chairs set, no. 17201, some seated figures, some standing figures at the rear where the bar is, "hardwood flooring" printed off the computer—flooring ads that I scaled down—and a couple of fish restaurant interior pictures. I found these on the internet, and they represent what you might see in a casual fish restaurant. The final touch are the red gingham tablecloths. Like the other images, I got them off the internet and scaled them down to fit the Preiser tables. This adds some authenticity and color, as I imagined how a crab restaurant might be decorated inside. I lit the scene with a single stick-on LED from Woodland Scenics' Just Plug line.

2. I fashioned the roof to be removable by grasping the blue trim at the back. That piece of trim is cemented to the roof but not the rest of building in order to be able to easily remove the roof and access the interior. When the roof is in place, you can't tell that this trim piece isn't cemented to the rest of the trim. One other point on lighting the interior: The LED is attached to the piece of styrene protruding out over the center of the scene. If you're lighting interiors it's helpful to have the light directly over the interior scene as opposed to having it in the back of the scene. This gives a more realistic look.

3. After the trolley drops passengers off at Supreme Crab, it makes one more stop before leaving the area. As it exits, the trolley passes the odd-shaped park which

I modeled based on an article by Gerry Leone. I first considered the Fog City Diner, but the space was too awkward for it to fit, so I opted for a scenic filler—grassy areas and trees. In addition to adding color and greenery, the trees help divide Fisherman's Wharf from the downtown area. I used Woodland Scenics ground foam in assorted colors and Scenic Express trees.

2

3

1

Dave Simon

2

3

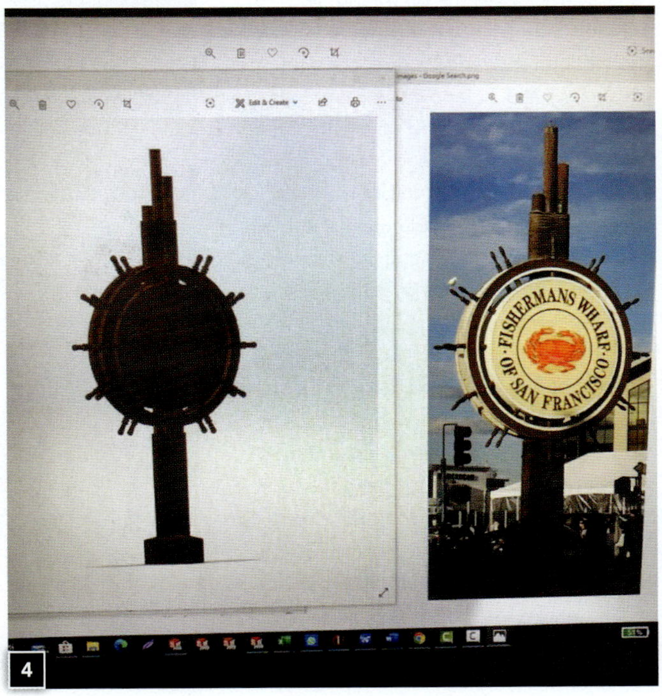

4

Waterfront

1. The foreground part of the scene is the waterfront. When I first installed the benchwork, I had left room for the waterfront, but didn't have a clear picture of what I wanted. This is often the case—it's normal to change plans or adjust the footprint as you move along. About halfway through the project we took a trip to San Francisco to visit family, and it was then we discovered the Chowder Hut restaurant. What a great place to grab a bowl of clam chowder! I also liked the building's distinct features—the octagonal shape, the frame sign above the entrances, and especially the tarnished copper roof in that verdigris blueish-green color.

2. Chowder Hut became a must-have for the layout, which then meant a small benchwork adjustment to accommodate it. I first laid out on craft paper the basic design.

3. Following the new design, I added a sandwich of plywood and Homasote and secured it in place. It's always a good idea to build flexibility into your original plan.

4. Chowder Hut and the big Fisherman's Wharf sign are 3-D printed. I worked with a local CAD designer—Scott Tarcy (info@caddesignhelp.com). It's an interesting process. I had given Scott a photo of the Fisherman's Wharf sign and assumed that a man in the photo at the base of the sign was 6 feet tall. From the photo and using that assumption, Scott created the design. This is a screen shot of Scott's computer and you can see the comparison of the model and prototype.

I learned there are alternatives in the printing process itself. To save on cost, I chose a less expensive method that sometimes leaves striated lines, which happened with the Chowder Hut roof. This required a bit of plaster and sanding for a smooth look. I also wanted a more defined set of ribs for the roof than was created in the printing process. I installed new ribs using .030"-square styrene. These are a bit oversized in appearance, but this made them easier to work with.

I painted the Fisherman's Wharf sign and Chowder Hut using traditional methods, but the roof on Chowder Hut required extra care. Here, I experimented with different techniques, and this is where I landed, again with the help of a YouTube video. I first applied a rust/brown undercoat, then added a weathered black wash followed by the verdigris color, Acrylicos Vallejo Verdigris Glaze, 70.832. I finished the roof with gray chalk streaks I applied with my fingers. It's good to experiment on scrap material first—but eventually I was satisfied with the look. The Chowder Hut roof is the most important part of the structure as it is so distinctive looking. Normally I shy away from using washes and chalks too heavily, but there's really no way to simulate the Chowder Hut roof without moderate to heavy weathering. To finish the roof, I installed the two Chowder Hut frame signs that I had custom made.

Dave Simon

5, 6. Crab Station and Gram's Lighthouse reflect a vibrant row of restaurants near Chowder Hut. Here I deviated a bit from my prototypical approach. My wife, Lisa, has been so supportive of my playing-with-trains time that I convinced Nick (of Nick's Lighthouse) to sell the business. Our granddaughters' "Gram"—that would be Lisa—took over the operation, and changed the name of the restaurant. She also decided it needed a remodel, and she's happy the JL Innovative café diner interior detail set spruced up the joint.

I added three tables and chairs, each with an orange-painted umbrella (noted from the overhead Google maps shot) that mimics the outside eating areas around Chowder Hut. With other figures and vehicles, the waterfront is bustling.

7. One last little detail (aside from the wharf and ship) is the parking kiosk. Like the other parking lot, there's an entrance gate but I didn't have enough space to fit this in without it looking out of place, so I opted for only the payment kiosk where visitors pay for their parking. Without the parking gates, the Preiser figures have to settle up using the honor system, and the last time I checked, I found they're trustworthy.

8. Building the Campbell wharf was enjoyable. It had been about 30 years since the last Campbell kit I built, and these kits are still terrific. After so much scratchbuilding, it was nice working with precision-cut parts and a full set of instructions. If you're familiar with this kit, you'll notice I only used about half the parts (due to available footprint issues) but I did find use for a few of the remaining pilings by building the little fence at the end of the parking lot preventing cars from going overboard into the water. I cut the pilings at a slight angle, drilled a hole near the top of each piling, stained them brown, and then threaded a small A-Line link chain to create the effect.

8

I spent a lot of time thinking through the sea wall as it's one of the first things you see and serves as a backdrop for the waterfront. I decided to create three distinct sections. I used Woodland Scenics cut-stone retaining wall parts for the wall that runs parallel to the edge of the layout. I only used the main part of the wall section and then used a wood piling to hide the seams between sections. I also used spare decking pieces and taller pilings from the wharf kit for the "inlet" part of the sea wall. I did a pilings-only section adjacent to the stone wall, and a wood retaining wall for the section adjacent to the wharf. I added a bit of green grass Woodland Scenics fine turf to represent seaweed and moss. The boat is from Sea Port Model Works. The company has a good selection of interesting-looking kits, and I chose one that grabbed my attention. One last point—when I test-fit the wharf and boat I decided to extend the benchwork about 6" as I thought the wharf and boat looked cramped.

To create the water I followed the techniques outlined by Dave Frary, describing how he developed the diorama he built for Sea Port Model Works. I reviewed several instructional videos for creating water, and thought his approach looked the most realistic. Two other advantages of his method are important—it's easier to control (no mixing or pouring) and a much lower cost. Click on the Sea Port Model Works website (seaportmodelworks.com) to see the video.

Final thoughts

This has been a wonderful project to finish the layout. I got great satisfaction by staying close to the prototype and modeling actual buildings and scenes. That helped me stay motivated. One other unanticipated benefit of modeling the prototype is that it's easier. You have a starting point—the actual scene—which I found enabled me to imagine what a 1/87 depiction could look like.

Learning new tricks on modeling the little things that help bring a layout to life—like the chain link fence—was also very rewarding. The internet is full of information, and a little extra time spent exploring different techniques can be very beneficial.

Hopefully you'll get some ideas for scenes you'd like to model by seeing how I approached Fisherman's Wharf. And above all, remember that famous motto—model railroading is fun!

CHAPTER THIRTEEN

Scratchbuilding a brass locomotive

By Andrew Dodge // Photos by the author unless otherwise noted

This 1888 builder's photo of a Baldwin Colorado Midland Ten-Wheeler offers plenty of useful information. Notice the air reservoir tank under the cab, which will be upgraded to a larger tank on the fireman's side in front of the cab as seen in the photo of the model. *Mel McFarland Collection*

Two O scale models of Baldwin Ten-Wheelers wait at the Basalt, Colo., coal dock on Andrew Dodge's Colorado Midland layout. All of his locomotives are scratchbuilt.

Building a brass steam locomotive from scratch might be considered a daunting task, but the process and results can provide those who love precision the ultimate in satisfaction. While this article concerns a class of engine built more than 100 years ago, the processes and techniques I used would apply to any brass locomotive project.

My first effort in scratchbuilding a steam engine was to re-create in On3 the Denver, South Park & Pacific's engine no. 1, the *Fairplay*, followed by constructing 13 Colorado Midland Proto48 steamers. Since delving into such a project is so far removed from opening a box with cast, cut, or formed parts, one should consider working up to it in stages before taking on what many consider the ultimate in model building.

A quote by Ray Davis comes to mind that applies to this type of endeavor: Patience is not passive waiting. Patience is active acceptance of the process to obtain your goals and dreams. Napoleon Hill puts it another way: Patience, persistence, and perspiration make an unbeatable combination for success. Before starting, I will give you one more piece of invaluable advice I learned as a Pontiac engine mechanic: Never put together something mechanical you cannot take apart.

1

Achievable goals

1. Preliminary steps are advisable. Working from something on the beginner level and then delving into an intermediate project would be a good method of learning the basics before doing your "graduate" project. Kitbashing should be considered as a first step.

The tools needed at this level should include not much more than the basic workbench items and maybe a 6" or 12" measuring caliper, which will be needed for more advanced projects. When you start doing some serious brass work, I would suggest getting a resistance soldering tool, some machining tools (which will make life easier), doing some internet searches for parts, and turning off the TV.

One of the first steps I took while working up to scratchbuilding an engine included a major facelift on this Bachmann engine. The cab was filed down to a flat surface and then layers of black walnut were applied to the exterior.

On the tender, some modest reworking was performed on the truck sideframes and extra detail added on top of the bunker.

A higher level of work on the boiler area included the addition of new domes and smokestack, which I made myself on a lathe. If one is not up to that level, these types of parts are commercially available as are the headlight and pilot I used.

2. The next level of engine rebuilding, which was the creation of the South Park's *Dillon*, was a quantum step up from the Bachmann. This entailed cutting up a shotgun type of boiler and making it into a wagon-top type. For those not familiar, the shotgun type is made using a straight sheet of brass bent into a tube. The wagon-top is the type where the firebox area has a larger diameter with a tapered section between it and the forward area that connects with the smokebox.

Taking a saw and cutting a perfectly made boiler took some intestinal fortitude, but once cut, it was a simple building project to complete the new boiler. If you decide to do a wagon-top boiler, the flared section will require several test fittings. I used heavy paper stock before going to brass. Be aware, you are not building a cone. The boiler is flat across the bottom with the top of the boiler having the biggest angle of the flared area. Remember Hill's quote I used, because it applies here concerning persistence and patience.

Besides the cosmetic boiler work, I had to make new drivers and tires because the factory driver centers had "rotted," and the wheels just spun around on the axle. However hard this was, I still did not have to machine a frame and construct a matching boiler and cab.

2

Building a frame requires the modeler to create an exact and detailed rendition of the mechanical part of the locomotive that is the heart of its ability to operate as a smooth piece of machinery. The rest of the engine has to match the drivers and cylinders to make a complete package. One can always use the frame and drivers from a commercial model at this intermediate phase of building a locomotive.

Developing a plan

The best advice when contemplating building a brass locomotive is to find an engine you like, one you feel able to fabricate, and an available set of plans that you could acquire from a historical organization or which has been published in a magazine such as *Model Railroader*.

Since I am modeling the Colorado Midland in 1897, I would have to rely on various sources such as photographs, plans printed in *Model Railroader*, and Baldwin specification sheets available online at Southern Methodist University.

The Baldwin records, however, leave much unstated, which required a great deal of photo analysis. To succeed in that arena, the modeler will have to have access to good photos showing the various aspects of the locomotive from right-angles.

3. All too often, photographs show the engines at angles that make it almost impossible to develop a reliable set of measurements. In this particular image of a Midland 1897 Baldwin Consolidation, the angle presents some level of problems, but it proved useful because the size of the drivers are a known diameter, which allows the builder to come very close to calculating the height of the tender deck, the running board, and how much higher the cab is above the boiler because it is directly over the last driver, etc.

A machine that changes over time

An additional problem facing those who choose a prototype project is the evolving nature of the locomotive itself. Whenever contemplating modeling a prototype, be aware of the changes made during overhauls and upgrades.

Examples of these types of changes can be seen in the Schenectady-built engine, sister to the Baldwins, built in 1887. The alterations include swapping the positions of the sand dome and bell, changing the cab roof, new knuckle couplers, raised sides on the coal bunker to increase fuel capacity, and an operating snow scraper directly behind the pilot.

A Schenectady-built (1887) Ten-Wheeler of almost the exact same specifications as the Baldwins' sits on the Colorado City Turntable in 1899. *A. J. Hundhausen Collection*

1. Fortunately, several photos exist showing the Baldwin Ten-Wheelers I wished to construct. When analyzing this type of image taken at a right angle, it is a simple, straightforward process of calculations and measurements to determine sizes, dimensions, and placements of all the aspects of the locomotive, or any other item one wishes to model.

To accomplish this task, one must know at least one measurement. Since the drivers' size is known within an inch or two, all one has to do is use calipers to determine how many thousandths of an inch the diameters of the drivers are as seen in the image.

Take that number and multiply it by trial and error until you know what number you need as the multiplier to reproduce the size of the prototype's wheels. That multiplier can then be used to calculate the size and dimensions of all the other items on the engine.

In the case of the Baldwin Ten-Wheelers, the smokebox front also changed over the years from the original design in 1888 (left) to a more traditional Midland design in the late 1890s. *Mel McFarland Collection*

Example: Measure the height of the steam dome in the photo and then multiply it by your multiplier, and you will have a very accurate idea of its size. Because of issues of picture quality and slight variations in one's measuring ability, it would be prudent to do your calculations several times with each procedure done independently of all the others. Then, you can take the average if you keep getting slightly different numbers.

I followed this procedure doing a Midland water tank plus calculating volume issues and arrived at the exact size of their water tanks, as I discovered a few days later when I found the Midland's specifications sheets.

1

Mel McFarland Collection

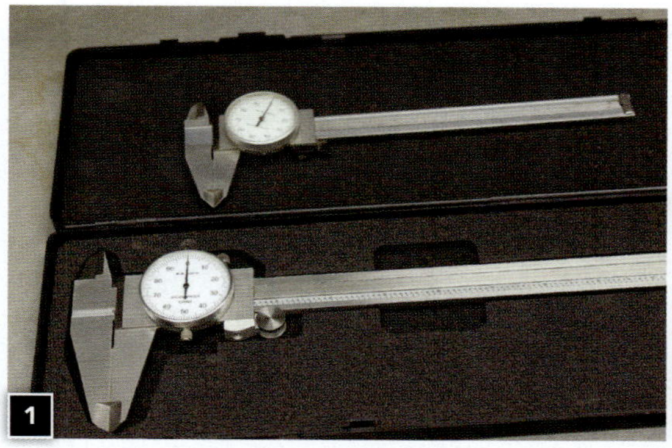

1

2

3

Materials

This brings us to the important issue of materials for the project. You can buy brass from a number of sources such as Online Metals, but like any metal, there are different alloys that have distinctive working characteristics.

For my On3 *Fairplay* project, I used K&S brass purchased from a local hobby supplier for the frame. It was a no. 260 alloy and very hard and more difficult to work with using hand tools. It was a thin material and worked well enough in the smaller size project.

I have since learned that no. 360 brass alloy is the best for model railroading work and machining in the larger scales. When selecting brass, your modeling scale will play a role in your decision making. HO modelers will likely have to choose similarly light and thin brass.

For all my O scale Proto48 locomotives, I used no. 360, 1/8-inch thick brass bar stock. When it comes to sheet brass, it will be of the no. 260 type and is available in various thicknesses. Last but not least, when doing tires, 12L14 round steel bar stock is an excellent product. It conducts electricity as well or better than other metals and is easy to machine. Stainless steel and nickel silver are best left for those who have a full understanding of their machining qualities.

Suggested tools

1. One of the standard questions any modeler will ask and which needs to be address is what kind of tools do I need? Good hand tools and files are important and should be found on most any workbench, but to be successful in building a locomotive frame, the modeler needs a 6" or 12" caliper for measuring. Micrometers are great but too difficult or impossible to use in many cases. Complete accuracy is required in almost all phases of this type of building process.

2. Some modelers have built locomotives with just a set of files and other hand tools. That is not easy, but doable if one has limited resources and lots of time and good hands. In order to make your life simple and ease all the handwork, I would suggest a lathe and a milling machine. These machines and their tools, drill bits, starter bits, mill ends, and measuring tools help turn long tedious tasks into a something much less difficult and with results of a much higher quality.

If you decide to purchase such machines instead of getting someone else to do the work, make sure they are of a size to do the projects you wish to build. Doing a project in O or F scale would require much larger machines than working in N scale.

I bought a Sherline lathe more than 20 years ago, and it still works just fine, but it would be too small for full-size O scale work. The plus and minus concerning the Sherline is that it is a proprietary company, but it offers an excellent selection of accessories.

3. Micro-Mark sells a nice quality mill. However, companies such as MSC have a far wider range of drills, starter bits, collets, and high quality German chucks that allow the modeler to perform the widest range of operations.

While being rather pricey, these chucks allow the machinist to use bits as small as no. 80 without breaking the bit. They are also easily removed, so you can go from mill ends to the chucks and back again via the collets. Because the mounting shafts on the chucks are straight, you do not have to force a tapered-ended chuck out of the machine, which can cause damage and alignment issues. As a final note, be prepared to spend as much on the accessories as the machines themselves.

Construction planning

1. Fabricating a model locomotive from scratch will require you to understand the multiple steps it will take to complete this type of project. In building a kit, all you have to do is follow a set of instructions one step at a time because all the planning has been done for you.

That is not the case with scratchbuilding. The modeler will have to be 5, 10, and maybe 20 steps ahead mentally of what he is doing so he will know how each step contributes to the final product.

I was once asked about where does one start? The answer? "Most any place you like." I have begun construction of the tender first, other times with the cab, and others with the frame. It makes little difference because you are going to build a locomotive according to a set of plans, which must meet exacting levels of quality so it will operate.

On this point, planning and construction of the frame must be done in conjunction with doing the bearings, axles, and driving wheels. Consider an automobile's engine: the block is cast and bored in one shop, the pistons are made in another, and the rods are made in another, but it all comes together to work as one unit. This is not hard to do once you understand the process and steps in building.

The builder should never start work without a detailed set of plans. Equally important, all measurements in this entire project will be in decimals. The frame, bearing, and driver issues all have to be done down to the thousandth inch range. Fractions are much too imprecise.

You must know where you are going and how and where each item on the locomotive will be located. Once you are happy with your frame layout, do your arithmetic. The old carpenter's saying of "measure twice and cut once" should be applied 10 times over in machining.

1

I always count forward and backward, from the middle out to each end, from each end, and so forth multiple times to make sure each set of calculations and methods used comes out with the same set of numbers. You cannot afford any errors, otherwise your frame will have to be redone, which no one wants to do.

The plan shown here was for a Consolidation, but all the measurements and positioning issues will be the same on any locomotive. It illustrates the need for accurate driver placement, i.e. spacing, and a ready reference in making the second side of the frame.

I found it is critical that each frame piece be made individually and be an exact copy of the first piece. In my time, I have built 13 locomotives using this method, which means 26 frame members, without a redo or an engine that would not operate. I will look at cutting a frame soon, but remember that even high-quality steel mill-ends deflect under pressure, making the bearing openings' side openings something other than square and exact if one tries to cut too much brass at one time.

2. Setting the cylinder position is another critical aspect of your model project. While there are variations depending on the engine's design, the cylinders on most locomotives must go directly under the smokestack and be forward and clear of the front driver's tires. Also, the height of the centerline of the cylinder has to be in line with the center of the driver axles or slightly above, never below, the centerline.

2

Mel McFarland Collection

Machining advice and rules

The setup of a lathe and mill is the most important and difficult part of any operation. All the calculations and various steps in machining a part must be taken into consideration before any work begins. Making the bearings required the use of both machines because each one had its own "task" to perform. Neither machine was used for any other job until all the bearings were fully machined and checked for complete uniformity. Never interrupt an operation with another job, otherwise your setup will be lost. You can never re-chuck a piece in a lathe and achieve the exact same setting. This issue is absolutely critical when doing the drivers.

The bearings

Once the frame plans are completed, machining the bearings is next on the agenda. Bearings of different sizes are commercially available if you would rather not make your own. I decided to make my own from no. 360 brass round stock. After drilling a hole just large enough to put a boring bar into the hole, I bored out the hole just large enough for the 3/16" drill rod to rotate smoothly in the hole. Boring is a must since a drill bit will "wander" and the hole will not be accurate.

Once bored (you can only bore out one or two bearings at a time), I turned the outside down to the size that would fit over the opening in the frame, and then machined the sides so they would fit nicely into the slots in the frame. (The frame openings or slots will be made only after all the bearings are finished and have exactly the same set of dimensions.) Examples of each phase of the process is shown in the photo. I used a piece of round bar stock to hold the bearings at exactly the same vertical height while cutting the lateral sides. The sides with the extensions will ride on the outside of the frame and will maintain it in place while keeping the drivers from being in contact with the frame. I also used a machinist's square to ensure both sides were perpendicular to each other. The final phase shows the almost completed bearing in the vise and with a mill end being used to bore out a hole for the coil springs. Now that I had the bearings and knew their exact size, I proceeded to cut the slots in the frames.

The frames

1. This is the stage where your detailed drawing of the frame comes into full play.

Following your plans, cut your two frame parts to length. When starting on the axle and bearing openings, I always start by cutting a smaller hole in the center of the space where the axle will be located. Referring to the space in the plan, I then set the caliper and lock it in place to the distance listed on the plans between the rear end of the frame and what will be the backside of the rear bearing opening. Cut open the bearing slot to the distance between the end of the frame and the squared opening for the bearing just big enough that the points of the caliper slide down into the bearing opening and the rear end of the frame like a warm knife into soft butter. No forcing and no loosey-goosey, this will be an operating machine. The front side of that bearing opening should then be enlarged just enough for the axle bearings to slide in and move up and down, and again no forcing and no loosey-goosey. Once finished, repeat the process for each additional axle opening, still using the end of the frame as your measuring point, NOT the preceding bearing opening. The exact process is followed for the other frame.

Before leaving the frame work, a word of caution. If you are using brass bar stock or some other metal, do not open the bottom of the frames where the bearings are located when first cutting your bearing openings. (Reference photo 1 below and the piece in the vise) The frame must be rigid enough and ensure that there is still sufficient material left on the bottom so the brass will not bend, but large enough to make sure the bearings fit and move smoothly up and down in their slot. Once you have cut a set of holes large enough to accommodate the bearings and completed all the other machining, (Reference photo 1 and the piece on top of the rear jaws of the vise) you have to construct bearing caps that will be secured to the bottom of the frame. Tap and bolt the caps to the underside of

1

2

3

the frame. On this small O scale engine, I used 0-80 hex-head bolts, which fitted nicely in the 1/8" piece of brass.

2. The photograph shows the front driver bearing with its spring, the frame, and the bolted frame caps with the heads of 0-80 bolts resting on the vise. Remember, you will have to take this apart a number of times, so do it well. Once the cap is bolted to the frame then and only then, can you open up the bottom of the frame so the bearings are in contact with the caps and can slide out through the bottom of the frame. Otherwise, the brass frame will bend, and it will no longer be true. The bolted caps will keep it true.

3. After checking that all the bearings fit the slots properly, solder both frame pieces together ensuring that the frame is perfectly square. I used a machinist's square and clamped the pieces together by the rear end of the frame before applying the solder. All the bearing openings are measured from the rear of the frame, so squaring the frame from the rear is an absolute must so the drivers and axles are all square to each other (photo 3 shows the nearly completed frame). Also be mindful of how wide you make the frame. It and the bearings must fit between the inside surface of the drivers and still have a little play from side to side and be able to move vertically when the springs compress. Be careful you do not make the frame too narrow or the locomotive will have another set of problems, "slop."

The drivers

With the completion of the frame, the modeler has to make the drivers, and you are now in for a modeling and machining experience where precision is every bit as critical as the frame. There are companies and individuals who have the needed tools and materials and who can make your parts, for a price.

The NMRA supplies all the specifications on its website under Standards - S-4.2 for all wheel configuration issues. Certainly before you even begin doing a construction plan, you are going to know the size of the drivers. Castings can be acquired from a number of suppliers, including Protocraft and Precision Scale, along with a lot of other parts in various scales, but the modeler is going to be limited in their selection, including diameter, number of spokes, types of centers, and counter-weights. This issue should be addressed during the selection process because if you cannot buy or make your own, you are going to be out of luck.

I purchased my cast centers from Precision Scale and was able to machine and do some modification work so they would fit my prototype. My approach to

1

making the drivers, which was passed on to me by Tom Mix (not the movie cowboy), is to first determine the distance across the face of the prototype driver from tire face to the opposite tire face.

You then measure the diameter of the casting of the driver center and how much they will be turned-down on the lathe, that of rims that will fit onto the completed wheel centers, and the tires, which will fit onto the rims and reproduce the scale size of the prototype drivers. I made three separate units: driver centers, rims, and tires, which will all fit and pressed together as one unit. In constructing the rim pieces, I took solid brass round stock and bored it out and cut the outside diameter to the predetermined size with all rims being the exact same size. The final product looks like a big ring and can be seen in the photo 1 at the bottom of the opposite page, sitting on the cross axis of the lathe.

The tires are made in a similar fashion. The large piece sitting on the axis shows what the drill bit removed in the center, then the recessed area cutout from the drilled opening to the next surface was bored. This inter-circular ridge will be pressed onto the rim. The outer edge of that ring will be the outer edge of the flange. (The wider area left was just the original piece of the bar stock that was in the jaws of the lathe.)

Before cutting this type of piece from the bar stock in the chuck with a cutoff tool, I will machine and dress what will be the face of the tire. The finished rim and tire will then be pressed together as seen in photo 1 on the left. Don't use too much pressure in the pressing process since both pieces are thin and easily deformed, a lesson I only needed to learn once (see Table 1).

During the design stage, you must also consider how to insulate the drivers on the fireman's side. Since I was creating a rim and tire unit and the insulating material would go between the rim and tire, I cut that set of inside openings on the tires a little larger to accommodate the insulating material. I have used Mylar, but styrene should work as well.

The tire/rim unit will be lightly pressed together. If the rim and tire don't seem to have a tight enough fit, or you are concerned about the stability of the insulated tires, you can use Loctite 680. It is a liquid that can be purchased from MSC and comes in a small bottle with an applicator end. Be careful, because it will set very quickly and can be "permanent."

With the tire and rim assembled, use an ohmmeter to ensure the parts to be used on the engineer's side of the engine conduct electricity. Follow the same procedure on the fireman's side and ensure the parts don't have any electrical flow.

Once the tire and rim pieces to be used on the fireman's side have been satisfactorily checked, take some clear nail polish and coat the front and back surfaces of the tire/rim assembly around the insulating material. Several coats would be advisable since you need to make sure no metal shavings etc. get into the space and allow electricity to arch across the insulation.

When machining the tire, I cut into the area that will be the face of the tire with a standard cutting tool down to the diameter of the finished wheel while leaving what will be the flange uncut. At this stage, I will have the face of the tire facing the tailstock, a 90 degree angle which will be the tire's surface, another 90 degree angle up for the flange, whose thickness will be determined by NMRA standards.

To finish the tire and put all the correct angles and curves in place, I mount my facing bit and carefully and slowly dress the final surface of the tire. If you wish and can find a supplier such as Protocraft with the correct tire sizes, you can purchase this item instead of making your own. Just making the tire facing tool took an entire afternoon.

Table 1: **Case Study for O Scale 52 Inch Drivers:**	
Distance from tire face to opposite tire face	**1.083"**
Distance from the edge of one flange to the opposite flange edge	**1.158"**
Inside diameter of the tire with no insulation	**.995"**
Width of the tire face for a flanged driver	**.100"**
Outside diameter of the rim	**.996"**
Inside diameter of the rim	**.905"**
Diameter of the cast driver center	**.905"**
Full width of drivers and tires	**.135"**

Machining and mounting the centers

The first step at this stage is to drill a hole in the center of the driver casting. This hole must be large enough to bore and smaller than the diameter of the axles to be used. (This hole will later be bored to accommodate the axles.)

Once done, you will have to make a tool that will be mounted in the chuck of the lathe. This tool will not be removed until all the steps presented in this section are completed. Initially, the tool you have to make will only concern the facing of the driver center and cutting the casting's outer radius.

Upon completion of all the facing operations, you will have to re-machine that same tool in order to finish the last step so the drivers can be mounted on the axles.

In making the tool, first select a round piece of brass with a larger radius than that of the finished drivers. Since the diameter of the brass piece is so large and needs to be very firmly secured in the jaws of the chuck, I created a nice-sized stud on the backside of the tool so it would go up into the hole in the center of the chuck's faceplate. This will preclude the cutting bit from "catching" the brass being machined and pulling the tool out of the jaws of the chuck.

Once mounted, machine the face of the tool so it has a perfectly flat surface while leaving a stud protruding out from the center. This stud will be a little shorter than the final thickness of the center casting for the driver. Also, the drilled hole in the center of the driver must fit smoothly but snugly onto the stud. With the stud complete, drill a hole in its center for tapping a 2-56 screw. I tapped a 2-56 hole in order that a screw with washers can be tightened down over the driver casting so as to prevent it from rotating while machining the faces of the driver castings.

After securing the casting with the face out, machine it to a finished surface. Once that is completed, turn it over and machine off the backside so the thickness of the casting matches the thickness of the rim/tire assembly you have already made. This thickness will vary according to scale and how close to prototype you wish it to be. When finished, you will have a nice set of front- and rear-surfaced castings.

In the next step you will remount the casting with the face out again. You will

1

also have to install two small screws opposite each other between the spokes, which will keep the casting in place while one machines the outside face to accept the rim/tire assembly.

After mounting the driver on the faceplate, carefully start cutting the outer surface and take it down just enough so the rim just fits onto the casting. This will be firm but not be a press fit, no loosey goosey here either, by any standard. Just like a hot knife going through butter.

Once all the castings are turned and there is a snug fit with the rims, the centers and tire/rim assemblies can be secured to each other on a flat surface on the workbench. Carefully solder them together with a resistance soldering iron or use something like Loctite 680. If you are going to use Loctite, follow the same procedure as described when securing the tires to the rims. Also, before using the Loctite to complete the assembly, make sure they will conduct electricity, which they should if you have the snug fit as described.

With the drivers assembled, we must now deal with trueing the hole in the center of the driver for the axles. Going back to the lathe and the tool that is still in the chuck, remove the stud used to hold the casting, and then drill a hole deep into the center of the faceplate and larger than the diameter of the axles to be used.

Working with a boring bar mounted in the tool post, cut into the faceplate just deep and wide enough to have the drive fit into the hole with the flanges protruding out over the faceplate. (See photo 1 above with the driver mounted on the faceplate secured by the chuck, and the brass piece sitting on the lathe's axis.)

There can be no sloppiness or too large a hole. The driver must fit exactly into the hole. If it does not, the driver can never be centered on the axle. This is also why the tires have to be the exact same size. Now install a driver with its tire face-first into the hole and secure it with two small screws through the spokes. Once in place, carefully bore out the center just large enough to accept a press-fitted axle.

Locating the position for the side rods is easily done once you know the stroke of the piston. Since the driver center has been bored and is ready for the axle, I made a brass tool with one end that will go into the axle hole and with a shoulder that sits on the face of the driver with a radius going out from the center equal to ½ the length of the piston stroke.

It is then a simple matter of scribing a line on the driver. Using a punch tool centered over the area where the side-rod will be attached, I then make a slight dimple for the drill bit. After drilling it out on a drill press with the proper bit for the bolt size you will use, you can tap the hole. You must be sure that the tap goes squarely into the hole.

A drill press, mill, or a self-made tool will be required to prevent the tap from cocking off to the side as it goes into the driver. Be aware that small deviations in angles can have huge consequences. The side-rod bolts must be perpendicular to the face of the driver.

When working on the drivers, the modeler must consider what kind of round, smooth surface to put in place for the side-rods to be secured to the drivers. When the rods rotate against a threaded surface they will cause the bolt to back out.

The modeler must create a smooth bearing surface for the side-rod journals. You could machine a piece that goes into the driver itself with a shoulder extending out for the side-rods. A retaining bolt would then go into the shoulder and secure the rod in place. This solution is what the prototypes use, but it is also the most difficult to reproduce in a model.

Another option would be to acquire bolts that are threaded where it goes into the tapped hole and smooth with no threading where the rods will sit. The last would be to make a smooth sleeve that goes between the bolt and the rod's journal box just long enough to keep the head of the bolt from tightening down on the journal itself.

Axles

The size of the axle is going to depend on the scale and size of your model. For my small, 19th century locomotives, I have always used 3/16" "air hard drillrod" from MSC. If I were building a Big Boy, I would use something quite a bit larger and similarly smaller axle for an N scale engine. Before making a choice, check your selection of gearboxes and see what diameter shaft they will accept. Don't go to your local hardware or big-box stores because their metal rods are not a top quality product manufactured for machine applications.

Drive train assembly

With your driving wheels, bearings, axles, and frame completed, it is now time for assembly. Although each operations is important, one of the most difficult and daunting is mounting the gear and drivers squarely onto the axles.

A press is strongly recommended along with some specialized self-made tools so one can properly and squarely press the parts together. I would suggest taking a piece of round bar stock a little shorter than the length of the axle and then drill a hole through the center just large enough for the axle to slide through. Then you can put the gear on the flat, base surface of the press, center the axle over the hole while it is in its sleeve, and slowly apply pressure with the press's arm.

You also might want to put a very small bevel on the end of the axle so it will start more easily into the gear and later the drivers. Remember that your baseplate and the sleeve have to have square and flat surfaces so the axle is pressed perpendicular to the gear and drivers.

Once you have the axle started into the gear and later the drivers, it is easy to follow the same procedure with other plates to center the gear, which is important and easily done with your measuring calipers.

Before pressing the drivers, make sure you have your bearing on the axles and in the correct orientation. Also, have the drivers quartered nearly where they will need to be. Quartering tools are available or you can make your own. Remember: The drivers must be quartered exactly or the engine's drive train will not rotate.

Cylinder saddles are available in a number of sizes, and you will want to buy or make yours when doing the plan for the frame. As shown in the photo above, it should be nicely in front of the first driver, under the boiler's smokebox and with the piston rod parallel to the rail and centered with the axles.

The design of the locomotive must be able to accommodate an electric motor with gearing on one of the driver axles. I have never liked seeing the gears or gearboxes between the frame and the boiler. Therefore, I have always designed my engines with the gearbox located on the last axle, which conceals it behind the firebox.

The motor is mounted on a plate that is directly bolted onto the gearbox. This eliminates any binding and just "floats" inside the boiler. The question of where to place the motor and gearing should be addressed in the design phase, not here and now.

The side rods are easy to make once you make a bar-tool the length of the drive train with bolt holes spaced exactly where the axles are located. You then drill and tap the bar-tool with the same size bolt holes that will be used on the drivers. This reproduces the exact spacing for the drivers and is important because the side-rods have to have that same exact spacing. Small adjustment might be needed, but be careful not to go too far with one side because that will impact the other. Now that all the driver train parts are assembled, the unit should roll nicely around on any flat surface or track.

The boiler

1. Fabricating a boiler requires the use of sheet brass (I used .017" for my O scale engines), some simple math, and the π formula. Several modelers in the past have asked about using tube metal for different applications in building a locomotive.

Tube materials are not the same alloy and are not fabricated in the same process as sheet or bar stock. You will find that unless it is an exact, usable size, it is not an option because it cannot be machined.

The first step in making the jacket would be determining the distance from the backhead in the cab to the back of the smokebox. That will give you the length. Determining the width of the piece will require the modeler to know the finished diameter of the boiler. Say the measurement across the boiler is 2 inches, then you multiply 2 inches x 3.14159, which gives you 6.28318 inches and thus the width of the sheet. Once cut, start to bend it around something like a piece of pipe or some other cylinder. To finish bending it, I use car radiator hose clamps that I keep tightening until it fits around the pipe.

After squaring the ends and making sure the backhead fits properly, one is ready to solder the two ends together. Don't forget to allow space for the gearbox and motor.

In order to get as perfect a circle as possible and keep the jacket from flattening out when cutting an opening for the mechanical part of the model, I made large rings out of brass, similar to the tires on a driver. These go inside the jacket. (In photo 1 you can see one at the backhead, one at the rear section of the flared area, and two more in the firebox that have been partially cut away for the gearbox and motor)

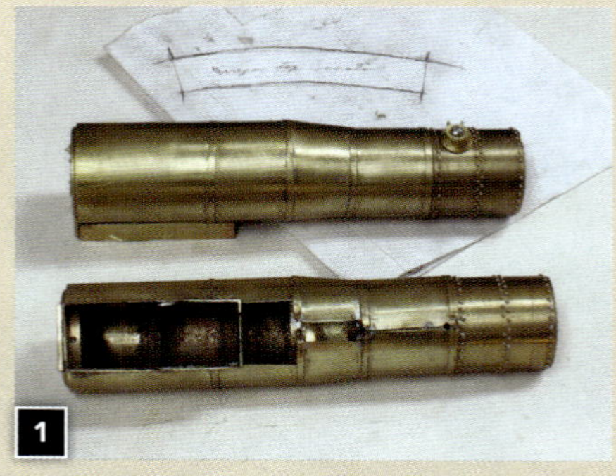

1

I placed one at the backhead, one just inside the front allowing for a small space for the insertion of the smokebox, and several others at various locations. After checking that the jacket is in firm contact with the rings, I solder the rings to the jacket before removing the clamps.

2. Fabricating the smokebox takes us back to the subject of tube materials. Again, don't, unless it is exact, and even then I would not suggest it. I use no. 360 round bar stock that I machine out the center and machine down the outside diameter to fit into the front end of the boiler jacket. This is why I placed the boiler ring slightly back from the leading edge of the jacket. You want the smokebox piece to just fit into the boiler jacket where you will solder the jacket and smokebox together.

3. The smokebox will be centered directly over the cylinder chest, and the petticoat pipe will be squarely above the nozzle, which exhausts the steam from the cylinders. All these parts could be glued, soldered etc. together, but don't. Tap and screw it together.

Why you may ask? Because it will have to come apart to attach your domes, which you can buy or make, and because you will have to deal with the motor issues throughout the life of the locomotive. Whatever you do, do not use any heavier or thicker brass than needed on the smokebox, or anywhere else, since it will act as a heatsink making soldering almost impossible.

4. Before leaving this part of the project, you must consider how to create the riveting commonly used on the smokebox. While "decal" rivets are an option, if one wants to install real rivets, a Rotary Table and Dividing Plate would make that job possible with excellent results.

The rotary table allows one to accurately rotate the smokebox in almost any number of divisions where you would use a starter bit to dimple the brass and then later repeat the process with a small drill bit. This is also where the Albrecht chuck earns its place in the workshop. Screws and rivets in the SAE and metric standards suitable for these kinds of projects can be found at model-motorcars.myshopify.com.

2

3

4

The cab

Another unit to fabricate for the locomotive will be the cab, which must fit the boiler and sit in the proper place in relation to the frame and the tender.

Unless you are constructing an engine with a lot of angles and curved areas, the fabrication process is simple and straightforward. It involves cutting sheet brass and placing additional applications of brass pieces on top of the base material and cutting holes for windows and panels that are recessed.

When I built my first Schenectady Midland engine, I did a layout plan twice the size of the model so I could achieve an exact, proportional replica of the prototype. Too many manufactured brass models failed to get the window and panel sizes correct, which marred the entire façade of the model.

The windows are cut out with strip brass representing the frame. The sill is just another set of pieces made up of narrow brass strips. If you want the roof to be removable, then you form the roof and solder small tabs or bars on the bottom of the roof section so they are in just enough contact with the inside of the cab walls to require some pressure to remove the roof. Having a removable roof is especially helpful when detailing the cab's interior and installing glass windows.

Domes

Domes on this period of locomotive are fairly easy to fabricate, while more modern ones such as those on one of the Virginian's 2-10-10-2s would be an entirely different project. One should create a drawing of the dome with all its different ridges, flares, curves, and rings before starting.

After determining all the distances and cutting a piece of brass round stock, it is placed in the lathe's chuck. I would then proceed to make square cuts into the side of the brass. When completed, you will have a piece with several different dimensional diameters with all the sides parallel with each other, no curved surfaces yet.

Using different types of cutting tools such as the ones shown in the lower area of the photo, you can start putting the curves onto the dome. Cutting must be done in very, very small steps and requires repositioning the tool post multiple times. You will be cutting on a broader surface than when using the usual cutting tool or boring bar. This type of procedure will thus create more drag on the piece being machined. Too much drag can cause the bit to bite into the work and ruin it or pull it out of the chuck. This same process can be done with the smokestacks.

Putting a radius curve on the bottom of the domes can be done several ways. The most difficult would be to do a mill setup and making a radius cut to match the curve of the boiler jacket. Sometimes doing projects the "correct" way is not practical.

I found the simplest and quickest method is to make the lower area of the dome a little longer, then use a Dremel tool to slowly grind away the underside to form the curved surface to match the jacket.

I have also bored out the underside so just a small shoulder remains and then use the Dremel tool. This takes some patience and many test fits because of this type of procedure and also because the boiler jacket is not going to be a perfectly curved surface.

The tender

The tender can be as challenging as the boiler and presents its own problems. Since the frame for a tender is rather straightforward and is constructed with heavier sheet brass for the deck and bar stock for the framing plus coupler and polling pockets, steps, lift-bars, bolsters, and other parts, I will skip this process and focus on the more difficult areas.

The tender bunker

1. The first step after determining the frame and bunker sizes is to cut a top and bottom plate for the bunker. They must be a matched set. Once the top and bottom plates for the bunker have been fabricated, the next item is to cut multiple sets of spacers set at the corners and midway point, which will give you the proper height and support your work.

I learned it was best to use spacers that were exactly the same size as the radius of the curves. Do not use solid brass round stock because of its weight and because that much brass will become difficult to solder. Squaring the bunker plates is an absolute if you want the wrapper to fit properly.

With the bunker frame done, you will have to return to your π formula to calculate the distance around all the curves (1/4 for the rear curves and 1/2 for the water legs). Double and triple check the distances along each straight side plus the distances of the curved sections because you don't want to spend time fabricating and riveting a sheet of brass and then find out it doesn't fit.

Carefully cut a sheet of brass the size needed for the entire wrapper, allowing for the flaring on the top, if applicable, and lay out your rivets.

1

2

2. Rivets can be made using real rivets if you are a really hard case. They can be simulated in the brass sheet with a rivet puncher of various types, which have to be done before attaching the wrapper to the bunker frame. Since they are commercially available, you could also use applied rivet decals after you have finished mounting the wrapper.

In my case, I made my own rivets and punching tool. While not the fastest and most interesting job, it was easy enough. The brass wrapper was placed on a piece of lead and the punching tool had a properly sized end to be pressed into the sheet.

To keep the punch shaft in place, I made the section that would go up against the jaws of the chuck larger so the shaft could not be pushed up into the chuck. It was then a simple process of moving the axis of the mill so many thousandths before pressing the next rivet.

It took a Sunday afternoon to do this with several breaks to keep from becoming "punch drunk" and bleary-eyed. That is how mistakes are made. When you make a mistake, remove the wrapper, place it on a flat metal sheet, and take a flat nosed punch and carefully flatten out the offending rivet. Then reinstall the sheet in the mill several rivets back from the mistake and test the alignment before redoing the mistaken hole.

When the wrapper is formed, riveted, and ready to be mounted, mark the exact center of the rear of the bunker frame and the same for that section of the wrapper. Align the marks and solder the rear areas together while not getting too close to the corner curves. (See photo 1)

Once you have soldered just the back end of the bunker along the top and bottom of the bunker frame, start to work the wrapper around the corners, the sides and around the water legs. Clamping is a must while soldering and keeping sure the bottom edge of the wrapper is flush with the bottom of the bunker frame.

3

After soldering the wrapper and bunker together, then you can bend the top flares into place. Since you cannot bend the flare around a corner, that portion of the wrapper has to be removed.

3. The wrapper for my *Fairplay* model shows what this looks like. To fill in the curved area, a small piece of sheet brass will have to be hand formed to simultaneously match the three areas that will be in contact with the wrapper, the two side flares and the bottom.

After carefully soldering the piece in place, a Dremel tool can be used to finish off the top so as to match the flared sides giving you a nice curved, flared corner. A piece of small brass wire can be soldered all along the top of the flared edge to give the tender wrapper a finished look.

To complete the tender's bunker, castings for the valves to feed water up to the engine can be placed near the ends of the water legs and a cross panel installed to indicate where the coal bunker ends. Water hatches come in a variety of sizes and types, and your fabrication or casting should match the period and type of hatch railroads used on your locomotive.

Trucks

The type of trucks used, like the water hatch, will vary with the weight of the tender, i.e. its size, capacity, and the time period modeled. Two- and three-axle trucks would be the most common and typically would be of a heaver type truck than those used on your typical freight cars.

Castings for these types of side frames can be obtained from part suppliers like Precision Scale. Be prepared to do some machining and drilling so the axles fit into the casting and the frames can be attached to the bolster.

Also be aware that the height of the trucks with the crossmember must be of the correct elevation so the tender deck is in alignment with the deck of the cab and the connecting floor plate.

In conclusion

After 60 days of work, my 1888 Baldwin Ten-Wheelers were completed and ready for the paint shop.

Completing such a project should give the builder one of the highest levels of satisfaction and joy. As stated at the beginning: Patience is not passive waiting. Patience is active acceptance of the process to obtain your goals and dreams.

Besides the pride, you can also submit your work for review for the NMRA's Achievement Program in Engine Building, and depending on your locomotive selection, you can earn points toward Prototype Modeling.

In writing this chapter, please keep in mind that there are a number of more or less cosmetic operations I did not examine. It would be next to impossible to do a full summary on a project that took me almost 60 days of full-time work to construct. My objective was to cover all the crucial mechanical and structural elements one needs to master to an operating steam locomotive.

Don't be intimidated by the multiple steps needed for each phase of the construction process. My best advice would be to break everything down into doable and understandable units, baby steps, and take a full set of notes. Machining can be infectious, and you will probably want to do another build. The rewards are immeasurable, so please consider joining the club of scratchbuilders.

CHAPTER FOURTEEN

Engine no. 18 in Kingfield

by Lou Sassi

Sandy River Railroad no. 8 rounds the curve as it heads into Phillips, Maine, inspiring Lou Sassi to create a similar scene. *Surman Collection, courtesy Jerry Devos*

This scene on Lou Sassi's On30 Sandy RIver & Rangely Lakes layout evokes Maine's 2-foot gauge railroads.

My cover photo on *Great Model Railroads 2020* was inspired by a photo of Sandy River no. 8 (later to become Sandy River & Rangeley Lakes no. 19) I discovered on page 91 in Jerry Devos' hardcover book *The Sandy River Railroad & Predecessors Volume 1*. The head-on view of that locomotive with its fireman sitting on the sill of the cab window as his train rounded the main line into Phillips, to me, captured the essence of narrow gauge railroading.

Look more closely and you can see the discarded barrels and wheels on the left along with the lone wooden box sitting in the dirt just to the right of the train. Although the rails, ball signal, water spout, section house, and sundry railroad details disappeared long ago, a trip to Phillips today will reveal that the period houses in the background still stand.

In my photo, engine no. 18 is leaving Kingfield on the curve to Strong. The fireman is straining to see the main line ahead as his train gains momentum. Fencing separates the railroad from the dirt road into Kingfield on the left, while the discarded ties to the right indicate that the maintenance crews are still at work even though it is 1934 and abandonment is approaching.

WHAT'S IN THE PHOTO

1. Right-of-way fencing
2. Dirt road
3. Discarded ties
4. Discarded barrels and wheels
5. Wooden box
6. Ball signal
7. Water spout
8. Section house
9. Period houses

BRING YOUR LAYOUT TO LIFE!

Realistic Layouts: Use the Art of Illusion to Model Like a Pro

Capture the feeling of the real world in miniature! This book will help you refine many areas of your layout, covering topics such as scenic elements, structures and the aesthetic of the overall environment.

#12828 • $21.99

Time Saving Techniques for Building Model Railroads

Building a model railroad – especially a room- or basement-sized layout – takes a lot of time. Tony Koester shares many invaluable time-saving tricks he's learned over the decades.

#12817 • $21.99

Workshop Tips & Projects for Model Railroaders

A compilation of insider tips and projects from *Model Railroader*, covering tools, painting and decaling, weathering, track and wiring, structures, scenery, locomotives, and freight cars in a friendly, knowledgeable style.

#12475 • $19.99

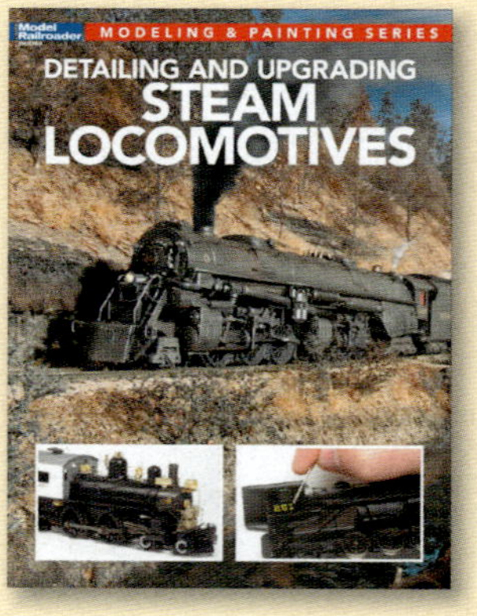

Detailing & Upgrading Steam Locomotives

This book offers you a single reference guide for upgrading, detailing, modifying, and maintaining your steam locomotive models.

#12812 • $21.99

Kalmbach Media

Buy now from your local hobby shop!

Shop at KalmbachHobbyStore.com